Lincoln Christian College

The Moore College Lectures 1980

THE SERMON UNDER ATTACK

D0813707

The Moore College Lectures 1980

THE SERMON UNDER ATTACK

Klaas Runia

EXETER
THE PATERNOSTER PRESS

Copyright © 1983 Klaas Runia

All Rights Reserved. No part of this publication
may be reproduced, stored in a retrieval system, or
transmitted, in any form or by any means, electronic
mechanical, photocopying, recording or otherwise,
without the prior permission of
THE PATERNOSTER PRESS

AUSTRALIA
Bookhouse Australia Ltd.,
P.O. Box 115, Flemington Markets,
N.S.W. 2129.

SOUTH AFRICA
Oxford University Press,
P.O. Box 1141, Cape Town.

This book is sold subject to the condition that it shall
not, by way of trade or otherwise, be lent, re-sold,
hired out, or otherwise circulated without the
publisher's prior consent in any form of binding or
cover other than that in which it is published and
without a similar condition including this condition
being imposed on the subsequent purchaser.

British Library Cataloguing in Publication Data

Runia, Klaas
    The sermon under attack.
    1. Preaching
    I. Title
    251   BV4211.2

ISBN 0-85364-341-5

Typeset by Photo-Graphics, Honiton, Devon
and Printed in Great Britain for The Paternoster Press,
Paternoster House, 3 Mount Radford Crescent, Exeter, Devon
by A. Wheaton & Co Ltd, Exeter.

CONTENTS

Preface   vii

1. Contemporary Criticisms   1
2. What Really is Preaching?   18
3. Preaching and the Bible   37
4. Preaching and the Situation of the Listener   57
5. Relevant Preaching   73
   Appendix: Women in the Pulpit?   97
   Index of Persons   109

68143

PREFACE

In 1980 the Principal and Faculty of Moore Theological College at Sydney, New South Wales, Australia, invited me to give the Annual Moore College Lectures. Having been a resident of Australia from 1956–1971, as professor of systematic theology in the Reformed Theological College at Geelong, Victoria, I gladly accepted this invitation. What a splendid opportunity to visit this wonderful country again and to renew our contacts with so many good friends. Above all, however, I felt greatly honoured by the invitation itself. Moore Theological College is one of the leading Evangelical colleges in the Southern hemisphere.

It was a rich experience to meet the faculty members and students of the College. My wife and I deeply appreciated the warm hospitality shown to us by the whole College community, in particular by the Rev. and Mrs. Bruce Winter, who offered us the hospitality of their home. The interest and patience shown by the audience at Sydney were a great encouragement.

Finally I would like to express my indebtedness to my eldest son, David T. Runia, M.A., for his willingness to read the entire manuscript and to suggest many linguistic improvements. Naturally, the lectures as published here are my sole responsibility.

ONE

Contemporary Criticisms

More than seventy-five years ago P.T. Forsyth started his lectures on *Positive Preaching and the Modern Mind* with the words: "It is, perhaps, an overbold beginning, but I will venture to say that with its preaching Christianity stands and falls".[1] A little later he calls preaching "the most distinctive institution in Christianity".[2] I think that at that time very few people, at least within the Protestant churches, would have contradicted him.

Of course, in those days, too, there were critical voices. Many people were dissatisfied with what they heard on Sundays. But their criticism concerned the *kind* of sermon they heard, rather than the sermon itself, the sermon as an institution. At that point they would most likely have agreed wholeheartedly with Forsyth's statement that with its preaching Christianity stands or falls. It is therefore not at all surprising that Forsyth nowhere in his book of over 250 pages offers an *apologia* for preaching as an indispensable part of the worship service of the church. He simply assumes it.

This situation actually prevailed right up to the sixties of this century. Admittedly, throughout the whole period many critical voices could be heard. At times the criticisms were even very severe. After World War I, for instance, Karl Barth severely criticized the preaching of his day. In a lecture on *The Need and Promise of Preaching*,[3] in July 1922,

---

[1]P.T. Forsyth, *Positive Preaching and the Modern Mind*, 1964,1.
[2]*Loc. cit.*
[3]Originally published as 'Not und Verheiszung der christlichen Verkündigung', in *Zwischen den Zeiten*, 1922, pp. 1–25. Afterwards published in English translation (by Douglas Horton) in *The Word of God and the Word of Man*, 1928.

1

delivered to a meeting of Swiss Reformed pastors, he expressed his fears that even Protestant ministers hardly knew any more what preaching really is. People come to church because they believe that something stupendous may happen there, namely, that God is present in his Word. But, asked Barth, do they really hear the Word of God? Or do they hear rather the minister's ideas about the Word of God, either orthodox or liberal ideas? Do they hear what they should hear, namely, God's redeeming and liberating Word in the real situation of their life? Or do they hear rather what the minister thinks their situation to be, to which he then adapts his message, either in an orthodox or in a liberal fashion? These critical questions which Barth and his friends posed to the preachers of their day were by no means superficial, but cut right to the very heart of the problem. Barth's own theology was virtually nothing else than one massive attempt to rediscover the secret of true biblical preaching. The same was true of other theologians of that period. However profound the differences may have been between Barth and Brunner, or Barth and Bultmann, or Barth and Tillich, it cannot be denied that in their theology they were all basically concerned with the self-same question: how can we preach today, so that modern man may really hear the Word of God? The same is also true of such post-Barthian and post-Bultmannian theologians as Gerhard Ebeling, Ernst Fuchs, Paul Van Buren, Jürgen Moltmann, Wolfhart Pannenberg, and many others.[4] None of them really questioned or questions the necessity of preaching as an indispensable function of the church.

Since the end of the fifties and the beginning of the sixties this situation has changed drastically following the appear-

---

[4]Cf. the following statement of Gerhard Ebeling: "The basic structure of theology is given by the movement from past proclamation to present proclamation. Accordingly, the task of theology is directed on the one hand towards past proclamation – and indeed there is a threefold division in this, its historical reference: to the Old Testment as testimony to the provisional proclamation, to the New Testament as testimony to the conclusive proclamation, and to church history as testimony to the subsequent proclamation. And on the other hand it is directed towards present proclamation – and indeed there is a twofold reference in this, its systematic and normative task: to what is to be proclaimed (dogmatics) and to the process of proclamation (practical theology)" (*Word and Faith*, 1963, 425). Here *all* theology is defined in terms of proclamation!

ance of a new critique. This critique was not aimed just at the form or even at the content of the sermon, but the whole phenomenon of the sermon itself was being questioned. In an article of 1959 A. Niebergall spoke of "*a deep scepsis[sic], a consuming doubt about the task and method, the meaning and purpose of the sermon in general*",[5] and in his contribution to the Festschrift for Emil Brunner, also published in 1959, E. Schweizer asked the brutal question "whether or not the word 'preaching' has lost its original sound and has become useless".[6]

Now it cannot be said that similar questions had never been asked before. As a matter of fact they had. As early as 1880 the London *Times* began an extended discussion by asking: "Why not be content to worship only, when we go to church?". In 1890 a New England periodical created a stir with a symposium on: "Shall we go on preaching?" Around the turn of the century it was seriously questioned whether preaching would survive the new century. And in the 1920s a prominent Episcopal minister made headlines in the U.S.A. by demanding a "moratorium on preaching".[7] Yet the situation today is different from that in 1880, 1890, 1900 or 1920 on at least two counts. In the first place, those earlier criticisms were exceptions to the rule. Hence the great stir they created. Today they are coming from all sides, not only from the social scientists and communications theorists, but also from the theologians, and above all from the ordinary people in the pew. All question the usefulness and validity of preaching in our modern day. The second difference is that the criticism goes much deeper. It questions the very existence of the sermon as an essential and indispensable part of the church's life and worship.

In this first chapter we shall analyse the various points of criticism put forward by these parties.

☆   ☆   ☆

[5]A. Niebergall, 'Die Predigt als Heilsgeschehen', originally published in *Monatschrift für Pastoraltheologie*, 48 (1959), pp. 1–17; afterwards republished in *Aufgabe der Predigt* (ed. Gert Hummel), 1971, pp. 295–320. The reference in the text is to found on p.295,

[6]E. Schweizer, in *Der Auftrag der Kirche in der modernen Welt*, Festgabe für Emil Brunner (ed. by P. Vogelsanger), 1959, 15.

[7]Cf. George E. Sweazey, *Preaching the Good News*, 1967, 7.

We begin with the critique of the *social scientists*. It is not surprising, of course, that they have made a special study of the sermon. It belongs to their task to investigate the place and role of the various institutions within human society. It is quite obvious that the church is such an institution and that the sermon, in its turn, is an important institution within the church. In their investigation of the sermon the social scientists point to several important aspects.

1. There has been a tremendous *shift in the position of the church within society*. Until the industrial revolution the church was at the centre of society. This appeared not only from the fact that the church building stood in the centre of each village and town, but even more from the fact that the whole culture was centred around the church, which functioned as the guardian of religion. Since the Middle Ages culture and religion had been intertwined, and this situation had not really been changed by the Reformation. Even in eighteenth century England we can still discover that the message preached by George Whitefield and John Wesley affected whole regions; eventually it even led to a national change of attitude to God. But, of course, these great Methodist preachers worked in pre-industrial Britain![8] A very definite change set in with the arrival of the industrial revolution. This was the more so, because it was accompanied by the steadily increasing impact of the Enlightenment, with its strong emphasis on the autonomy of man. Indeed, one could describe the Enlightenment as basically a movement of emancipation, seeking to liberate Western man from the authoritarian shackles of Scripture and the church. The result of this combination of factors was a process of secularization which deeply affected Western society and which in our day seems to have been almost brought to completion. In the course of this process the church has lost its hold upon large sections of society, notably the working class and the intelligentsia. In the meantime the church itself has largely become a typical middle class institution, the impact of which upon society as a whole has become minimal. In addition, due to changes in the rhythm of life,

[8]Cf. Gavin Reid, *The Gagging of God, The failure of the Church to communicate in the television age*, 1969, 22.

Sunday is no longer the important day of rest and worship. "Between staggered work schedules, on the one hand, and more long weekends devoted to recreation, on the other, regular church attendance has suffered markedly, especially in urban and suburban areas".[9]Fewer and fewer people go to church and those who still do go often complain about the mediocrity of the sermons they hear.

2. There has been a tremendous *shift in our culture itself.* We already mentioned the continuing impact of the ideas of the Enlightenment, with their emphasis on the *autonomy* of man. Modern man who, to a large extent, is the final product of the Enlightenment movement, does not want to be told what is true and worthwhile, he wants to discover it for himself and, accordingly, he also wants to determine for himself what he should do. In Bonhoeffer's well-known phrase: man has "come of age". According to the social scientists this has far-reaching consequences for the sermon too. H.D. Bastian once put it thus: "Man not only has an ear, but a tongue as well!" Instead of being at the receiving end only he wants to join in the discussion. But the sermon provides no opportunity for discussion. As far as its structure is concerned, it typically belongs to the old paternalistic cultural pattern of the past, in which the preacher was the pastor who feeds his flock. But modern man does not want to be treated as a passive sheep that has to be fed. He wants to know *why* it is worthwhile to believe what the preacher tells him. He wants to hear arguments and then make up his own mind about their validity.

Moreover, believing is not a once-for-all happening, but a process in which the faith of the believer, by means of ever new experiences, continually changes and develops. In particular in our modern world with its abundance of beliefs, life views, ideologies, etc., the believer cannot make up his mind in a once-for-all decision, but to believe means to be engaged in what the German sociologist H. Schelsky calls a process of "Dauerreflexion", of continuing reflection.[10]

[9]Leander E. Keck, *The Bible in the Pulpit, The Renewal of Biblical Preaching,* 1978, 40.

[10]H. Schelsky, 'Ist die Dauerreflexion institutionalisierbar? Zum Thema einer modernen Religionssoziologie', in *Zeitschrift für Evangelische Ethik,* I (1957), pp. 153–174. Cf. H. Goddijn, *Sociologie van kerk en godsdienst,* 1966, 59ff.

All this means that modern man increasingly becomes impatient, when he encounters structures that allow him to be a spectator only. He wants to be regarded as a partner rather than as a dependent and subordinate follower. Accordingly, he demands structures of communication that offer scope for participation not only to officer-bearers, but to members of the congregation as well. It is obvious that, within this frame of thinking, discussion is a much more suitable means of communication than the sermon. L.E. Keck describes this contemporary mood as follows: "If something is worth communicating, don't spoil it by preaching it! Let it emerge in the give-and-take of the group; celebrate it by music, dance or drama. In preaching, people are as passive as chickens on a roost – and perhaps just as awake. For whatever reason, the authority of the preacher has become problematic."[11]

3. There is still another point of criticism often mentioned by the social scientists. Modern life, they say, has become *far too complicated* for a sermon prepared by one single individual. In pre-industrial society the minister probably knew all his parishioners and was acquainted with their overall situation: their family life, their working life, their recreational life (in as far as they had any!), etc. In most cases this is no longer so. The old situation may linger in some rural areas, but even there life is changing fast. Most people in urban and suburban areas live in various circles (family, job, club, church, etc.), which no longer overlap but are quite separate. Even a husband and wife often find it difficult to have a clear idea of what the partner is doing at his or her job. For a minister it is simply impossible to be acquainted with all these circles.

In addition, we are living in an age in which human knowledge increases at such a speed that no individual can keep abreast of all developments. Take, for instance, the increase of scientific knowledge. According to some experts, the knowledge of mankind doubled in the period between 1800 and 1900. In the next fifty years it doubled again. Since then it has doubled every fifteen years.[12] Now it may be said

[11]Leander E. Keck, *op. cit.*, 41.
[12]Wolfgang Bartholomäus, *Kleine Predigtlehre*, 1974, 13.

that it is not the task of the minister to know and speak about all kinds of scientific developments. This is undoubtedly true. Yet among his parishioners he may find people who are deeply involved in these developments, and should not he, as their minister, at least be aware of the many existential and ethical issues they face?

The problem is aggravated still more by the fact that the life of the minister himself is becoming so complex that there is hardly any time left for preaching and the preparation required for it. On the basis of an extensive study of the lives of 1,600 clergymen of twenty Protestant denominations all through the U.S.A. Samuel W. Bizzard concluded even in 1955 that the traditional role of 'preacher' in Protestantism is of "declining importance. It is being relegated to a less important position, and the roles of pastor, counsellor, organizer, administrator, and promotor are consuming the major portion of the minister's time."[13] How can a man in such a position deal with the concrete problems of his listeners, let alone with the many macro-ethical problems that vex our world? He most certainly cannot do it on his own, but needs the assistance of the members of his congregation who often know much more about these problems than he. In other words, there is hardly any place left for our traditional Protestant form of monologue preaching.

☆   ☆   ☆

Similar criticisms come from the side of the modern *communication experts.* They too are naturally interested in the sermon, because it is still one of the most common means of communication. Their evaluation and assessment, however, is largely negative.

1. They point to the great *changes* that in recent years have taken place (and that are still taking place) in the whole *structure of communication.* All kinds of new media have been introduced and each medium exerts its own influence

[13]Ilion T. Jones, *Principles and Practice of Preaching,* 1956, 28. Cf. Keck, *op. cit.,* 15.

upon its user. One of the merits of Marshall McLuhan has been that he has drawn our attention to this fact.[14] First he has pointed out that the invention of book printing brought about a tremendous change in the way people absorb information. The printed page presents its case in a logical, sequential, linear fashion. It requires concentration and appeals to and develops the rational in man rather than the intuitive.[15] The Protestant sermon started shortly after the invention of printing and it is no coincidence that it showed similar characteristics. It too placed much emphasis on the logical, well-developed argument and also appealed to man's rational rather than his intuitive faculty.

In our day, however, the new mass media, such as the modern popular newspaper, advertising and television, have become dominant in the Western culture (and at tremendous speed the same is happening in the non-Western cultures). McLuhan has charcterized these new media as 'cool', over against the older ones as 'hot'. A book is a typical example of a 'hot' medium. It presents much material, which as we have seen, is set out in a clear, logical fashion. It requires little interpretation, but does demand concentrated attention. Television, on the other hand, is a typical example of a 'cool' medium. Although it also presents much material, it does this in quite a different way. It dumps a mass of facts and pictures into the lap of the viewer, requiring him not to search for the information, but rather to select from it whatever appeals to him. Putting him, so to speak, in the 'global village', it does not ask him to absorb a well-documented and well-ordered argument, but rather (as in the village of old) it invites him to participate in the process of learning that is set into motion by the non-linear presentation of the material.

It cannot be denied, I think, that there is a great deal of truth in McLuhan's analysis. Nor can it be denied that the modern mass media have deeply affected the way in which contemporary man obtains his information. "Indeed, in our

[14]Cf. Marshall McLuhan, *Understanding Media: The Extensions of Man*, 1964. Marshall McLuhan and Quentin Fiore, *The Medium is the Massage*, 1967. Marshall McLuhan and Quentin Fiore, *War and Peace in the Global Village*, 1968.
[15]Cf. Gavin Reid, *op. cit.*, 27.

schools today new teaching methods are exploiting the non-linear, non-sequential means of conveying information. The class room is becoming the village with learning gleaned from projects and a high degree of participation from the pupil."[16]

It is no wonder that communication theorists who believe that this development will continue and even be speeded up by the new electronic technology, have a rather low appreciation of the traditional sermon. It seems to belong to a past period. Like the book, it presents its case primarily in a logical, sequential, linear fashion and appeals to the rational rather than the intuitive in man. But the man to whom this appeal goes out has changed in the meantime. Although he still reads books, he essentially belongs to the new communication era, the era of the 'cool' media.[17]

2. There is, according to the communication experts, still another inherent weakness in the traditional sermon. It belongs to the very structure of the sermon that it is a *monologue*, a one-way communication. There is hardly any feedback. The preaching minister has no real means to gauge the reactions of his listeners and to make the necessary corrections and adjustments in his approach. H.D. Bastian says in his book *Verkündigung und Verfremdung* (Proclamation and Alienation) that preaching, because it is non-cooperative communication, is no longer suitable for our time. It is like using a kerosene lamp in the age of electric light.[18] Similar statements abound in present-day homiletical literature. Ilion T. Jones quotes Marshall L. Scott who, twenty-five years ago, at a meeting of the Association of Seminary Professors in the Practical Field, pointed out that in labour-industry relations "one-way communication ... is as outmoded as the model T", and added that traditional preaching will be less and less effective with men who are accustomed to two-way communication in other areas.[19] Of course, one can put it much more bluntly too, as in the following definition of the sermon: it is "a monstrous

[16]Gavin Reid, *op. cit.*, 31.
[17]Cf. Gavin Reid, *op. cit.*, 32ff.
[18]H.-D. Bastian, *Verkündigung und Verfremdung*, 1965, 58ff.
[19]Ilion T. Jones, *op. cit.*, 30.

monologue by a moron to mutes".[20] But however one formulates it, it all boils down to the same; preaching, as we are
used to it, has had its time.

It is not surprising, therefore, that recent years have seen
attempts to find new forms of preaching which may help to
overcome this inherent weakness of the traditional sermon.
Sometimes it is done in the form of a dialogue between two
persons during the worship service. In other cases members
of the congregation assist the minister in the preparation of
his sermon or receive the opportunity to ask questions after
the sermon has been delivered.[21] In this way, it is often
argued, we can also do more justice to the Reformation
concept of the priesthood of all believers.

3. Closely related to the foregoing two points is the third
point of criticism coming from the communication experts.
They point to *the low degree of effectiveness* of the traditional
sermon. Of course, this too is not an altogether new discovery. Already at the end of the nineteenth century Henry
Ward Beecher was complaining that "the churches of the
land are sprinkled all over with bald-headed old sinners
whose hair has been worn off by the friction of countless
sermons that have been aimed at them and have glanced off
and hit the man in the pew behind".[22] The modern communication theorist would agree with him, apart from the
last part. For he does not even believe that the man in the
pew behind is hit (if there is a man sitting there at all)!

I must immediately add that this scepticism as to the
effectiveness of preaching is not without foundation. Several recent studies-in-depth have shown that on the whole
listeners remember very little of the average sermon. In his
book, *The Empty Pulpit*, Clyde Reid states: "Preaching does
not communicate". "Testing lay persons from a number of
churches in the Detroit metropolitan area, Parsons found
that the intended content of the sermon is very poorly
communicated". He found that in meetings immediately
following the worship service, *fewer than one-third* of the
persons tested could give a reasonably clear statement of the

---

[20]R.E.O. White, *A Guide to Preaching*, 1973, 5.
[21]Cf. J. Daniel Baumann, *An Introduction to Contemporary Preaching*, 1972, 261ff.
[22]Quoted by Ilion T. Jones, *op. cit.*, 31.

primary 'question' of the sermon or the 'answer' suggested in the message.[23] In another research project the results were even worse: only 21 per cent of the 271 persons (who all felt that the sermon was either 'superior' or 'good') could reflect the minister's *central message* clearly and accurately.[24] A similar conclusion is reached in a Dutch study.[25] The author discovered that, even when people said they enjoyed the sermon, they quite often did not remember the content! At this point it could be objected that the cognitive level is not the only one to take into account. A sermon could well touch the listener on another level, for instance, the emotional or affective level. Undoubtedly, this is true. But one of the disquieting conclusions of the studies mentioned before is that on the whole sermons rarely lead to a change of mind or change in behaviour. Reid, for instance, is very pessimistic on this point. And he is not the only one, as appears from the fact that a conference of theologians in the U.S.A. also concluded that the sermon is "one of the least satisfying methods for extending religion's message to outsiders".[26]

☆   ☆   ☆

Unfortunately, we have not yet come to the end of our sermon litany. In addition to the social scientists and the communication theorists, there is still a third group of people who voice severe criticism of the sermon. Perhaps they are the most unlikely members of the critical choir, for they are *theologians*, i.e., preachers themselves.

Again the critique takes various forms.

1. Especially among theologians of the post-Barthian era in Germany (but also in other countries, e.g. the U.S.A.), there is a rather widespread *reaction against the high view of preaching* advocated by *Karl Barth* and other champions of the so-called Theology of the Word of God. The post-

[23]Clyde H. Reid, *The Empty Pulpit*, 1967, 29.
[24]*Op. cit.*, 30.
[25]C.J. Straver, *Massacommunicatie en godsdienstige beïnvloeding*, 1967.
[26]Clyde H. Reid, *op. cit.*, 32.

Barthian theologians do not deny that dogmatically Barth's view is correct. On the contrary, they agree with him that our preaching can become the Word of God only "where and when it pleases God". But what they reject is that this is all that is to be said about our preaching. In the Preface to a symposium about the theory and practice of preaching the authors begin with the following quotation from Gerhard Ebeling's *The Nature of Faith*: "We have to bring a certain measure of good will to the average sermon, if we are not to be bored or furious, sarcastic or melancholy in our reactions. What an expenditure of effort is put into the preaching of the Christian faith up and down the land! But – with exceptions – is it not the institutionally assured platitudes which are preached?"[27] The post-Barthians wholeheartedly agree with these words and draw the conclusion that we should stop taking our homiletical starting point in such beautiful dogmatic views. In homiletics we have not simply to assume that our sermons participate in the mysterious activity of the Word of God, but we have to take them seriously for what they really are: human attempts to communicate the Gospel. Homiletics is quite simply the study of this particular kind of communication, and as a kind of communication it has to be tested by the laws of the science of communication. If such a test shows that the sermon is a totally ineffective kind of communication, we have to accept the consequences and replace it by more suitable means of communication. Some, though not all, of the post-Barthians do indeed come to this conclusion. H.D. Bastian, for instance, even goes so far as to question the whole concept of the worship service. According to him we may have to look for entirely different forms of proclamation and worship.

2.   Another point of criticism, also coming from the side of the theologians, is that the traditional sermon is *far too introverted* in character. It concentrates almost exclusively on the religious needs of the individual member of the con-gregation, thus confirming and even supporting the social

---

[27]Gerhard Ebeling, *The Nature of Faith*, 1961, 15. This statement is quoted in *Zur Theorie und Praxis der Predigtarbeit*, Predigtstudien Beiheft I, edited by Ernst Lange (in cooperation with Peter Krusche and Dietrich Rössler), 1968, 8.

and political *status quo*, while in actual fact our world cries out for new social and political structures. According to the advocates of so-called *political theology*, the church should first of all act as an agency for social and political change. Christ's gospel of the Kingdom is primarily a call to break down the structures of injustice that abound in our world, and to work for a new world of justice and peace for all. Both the traditional sermon and the traditional worship service are inadequate for this purpose. We have to look for new, alternative forms. Some years ago Dorothee Sölle and her friends experimented with such new forms in Cologne. Instead of the ordinary evening service they held meetings in which the main emphasis was on information, discussion and planning for action.[28] There was no preaching, but all participants were free to make their own contribution, which eventually led to the formulation of a plan for action. These experiments, however, have been rather short-lived, most likely because they were too radical. More successful at present, at least in Europe, are the alternative congregations which call themselves "basis groups", consisting largely of politically motivated Christians. They do retain the idea of the worship service and of the sermon, but preaching is no longer the prerogative of the minister or the leader, and its main purpose is no longer the building up of the personal faith of the individual believer, but rather the preparation of the whole congregation for social and/or political action.

✧   ✧   ✧

So far we have mentioned three categories of critics: the social scientists, the communication experts and the theologians. But the main category has not yet been mentioned. That is *the man and the woman in the pew!* They are the people who more than any one else (with the exception of the minister) are involved in and affected by preaching. What do they think about the sermon? Usually their voice is

[28]Cf. *Politisches Nachtgebet in Köln*, edited by Dorothee Sölle and Fulbert Steffensky, Vol. I, 1969, Vol. II, 1971.

hardly heard. Here too we find a silent majority. But in this case silence cannot be taken to mean approval. In fact, there is much criticism among the listeners. Most of them do not object so much to the fact that preaching is still an integral part of the worship service, but they object to the *quality* of what they hear. Their main complaint is that many sermons are *so terribly boring*. Actually, this is the most crushing criticism of all! For let us face it, the church claims that its message of God's redemption in Jesus Christ is the most exciting message that has ever been proclaimed. Yet the people in the pew often feel utterly bored, when their minister speaks about this message. And since they have no real say in the matter – they are literally at the receiving end – they can make their disappointment and their dissatisfaction heard in only one way: by staying away!

Naturally, this is not the only reason for the current decline in church attendance and church membership. There are other factors as well. There is the growing impact of secularism. There is competition from the mass media and from recreational opportunities. There is also plain unbelief. Yet we should not underestimate the fact that many church people are deeply dissatisfied with the preaching of their minister. Apart from unbelief, boredom is the greatest enemy of the sermon.

☆   ☆   ☆

When we take account of all that has been said so far, we can only conclude that the situation is rather gloomy and that the future of the sermon does not look very bright. How bad it looks was brought home to me on Good Friday, 1980, when I listened to the Dutch radio. In the evening a Lutheran service was broadcast. It was a complete service, including the celebration of the Lord's Supper. Only one part was lacking: the sermon! The service of the Word was limited to two Scripture readings from the Gospel. For the rest there was much singing and praying, all leading to the service of the Lord's Table. But no sermon! I could not help

thinking of David's complaint after the death of Saul and Jonathan: "How are the mighty fallen!" (1 Sam. 1:19). I recognize that even today there are still many people who speak highly of preaching. But – the problem is that these people are usually theologians, i.e. preachers themselves! In his book, *The Renewal of Preaching*, published in 1969, David James Randolph says that the civil rights movement in the U.S.A. has brought to light again that "preaching is the pivot on which the Christian revolution turns".[29] On the first page of his book he even dares to suggest that "the tired criticisms to the effect that preaching is passé, that the day of the preacher is past, that preaching is merely an 'auxiliary' function of the church – all this prattle about preaching's being obsolete is itself becoming obsolete".[30] Another homiletician, J. Daniel Baumann, acknowledges in the introduction of his book, *An Introduction to Contemporary Preaching*, published in 1972, that there is much criticism of preaching,[31] but then replies with the personal testimony: "I have a profound faith in preaching".[32] He supports this testimony by pointing out that the Bible is on his side and that church history validates his faith in preaching. He further believes, with John Killinger, that "people are not tired of preaching but of non-preaching, of the badly garbled, anachronistic, irrelevant drivel that has in so many places passed for preaching because there was no real preaching to measure it against".[33] Other writers, usually theologians too, claim that if we had a revival of oratory, there would be a bright future for preaching. George E. Sweazey, for example, rejects the statement: "One-way communication is as outmoded as the Model-T", out of hand. He simply declares: "Apparently the author has not seen the papers", and then goes on to say, among other things, that "it was by endless oratory and public indoc-

[29]David James Randolph, *The Renewal of Preaching, A new homiletic based on the new hermeneutic*, 1969, 3.
[30]*Op. cit.*, 1.
[31]J. Daniel Baumann, *op. cit.*, 11. "Preaching is anathematized as boring, dull, uninteresting, irrelevant, void of courage, and incomprehensible".
[32]*Loc. cit.*
[33]The quotation is from John Killinger, *The Centrality of Preaching in the Total Task of the Ministry*, 1969, 21.

trination that the masses in North Vietnam, Cuba and China were made Communist".[34] I wonder whether Mr. Sweazey would still say this after reading in the papers of the many Cubans who have tried to escape from their communist paradise. Apparently this oratory was not very effective either!

I do not think that we can lightly brush off all these criticisms by suggesting some easy solution or by uttering beautiful phrases about the deep mystery of preaching. These criticisms have to be taken seriously, for the simple reason that they contain much truth. For example, it is a fact that our sermons often produce little effect. It is a fact that too often – to use the phrase of Ebeling – our sermons are little less than "institutionally assured platitudes". But, secondly, we have to take these criticisms seriously also for the sake of all those people who still attend our church services regularly. Kathleen Nyberg rightly observes: "When we consider the constant barrage of written and spoken words endured by modern man, one wonders with surprise about the large number of people who submit themselves Sunday after Sunday to the words of a preacher ... The sermon deserves to be taken seriously, therefore, and ought to receive first-class attention and labor".[35] And finally, there is still a third reason why we cannot and may not disregard these criticisms, namely, the fact that the decline or even dismissal of preaching would be detrimental to the life of the church. It has been rightly observed that the church has been most healthy when its pulpit was robust,[36]

---

[34]George E. Sweazey, *op. cit.*, 8.

[35]Kathleen Neill Nyberg, *The Care and Feeding of Ministers*, 1961, 104. In this book Mrs. Nyberg wrote to other ministers' wives and emphasized that there are periods in a minister's life when he needs undistracted time for his sermon preparation. In particular in our day, when people are exercising "much prerogative in the matter of what they will and will not hear", we must make sure that any decline in attendance at our preaching services is not due to a lack of "first class attention and labor" on our part. Cf. James Earl Massey, *The Sermon in Perspective, A Study of Communication and Charisma*, 1976, 32f.

[36]Cf. J. Daniel Baumann, *op. cit.*, 12. He quotes the following statement from H.C. Brown Jr., H. Gordon Clinard, and Jesse J. Northcutt, *Steps to the Sermon*, 1963, 28/29: "Whenever Christianity has made substantial progress, great preaching led the way. In the history of Christianity there have been five great centuries of growth and development. These same five periods are the five centuries of preaching: the first with the apostles, the fourth with Chrysostom and Augustine,

and that across the centuries, whenever the church has been vital, there was a strong emphasis on preaching.[37] All revivals, including the greatest revival of all time, the sixteenth century Reformation, were the result of vigorous, Bible-oriented preaching.[38] It is therefore of vital importance for the church of our day to engage in a heart-searching reflection upon its preaching.

This book is intended as a small contribution to this reflection. It will be evident that it is impossible within its short compass to deal with the problem in its totality. We shall concentrate on some major aspects. In the second chapter we shall ask the fundamental question: *What really is preaching?* The third and fourth will deal respectively with: *Preaching and the Bible*, and *Preaching and the situation of the listener*, while finally we shall consider: *When is preaching relevant?*

the thirteenth with Francis of Assisi and Dominic, the sixteenth with Luther and Calvin, and the nineteenth with Spurgeon and Maclaren. Contrariwise, whenever preaching has declined, Christianity has become stagnant. In the Dark Ages, in the fourteenth and fifteenth centuries, and in the seventeenth and eighteenth centuries, in most countries preaching was weak and ineffective."

[37]Cf. George E. Sweazey, *op. cit.,* 6f. "The flaming movements have been kindled and kept ablaze by preachers such as Ambrose, Augustine, Savonarola, Hus, Luther, Calvin and Wesley. Protestantism has never found a substitute for preaching, and it never can. Its whole life is bound up with the personal communication of Christian truth and guidance within the fellowship of worship. The health and vigor of a church will always be related to the health and vigor of its preaching".

[38]Cf. R.E.O. White, *op.cit.,* 7f. "The truth is, that Protestantism flowered in preaching, as has every great Christian movement. The great Awakening, the Evangelical Revival in England with Wesley and his band of preachers, the Welsh Revival and the Scottish, all soared into fine sermons. The whole modern missionary movement may look back with gratitude to a single sermon preached by William Carey at Nottingham in 1792...And the same is true of each great evangelistic renewal; names like Wesley, Whitefield, Rowlands, Haldane, Drummond, Sankey, Moody, Graham leave no doubt that preaching has its place in God's plan of redemption."

TWO

What Really is Preaching?

We have seen that today the sermon is under attack from many quarters. Social scientists, communication experts and even theologians—all join the critical choir. Each party has its own kind of criticism, but whatever the critique may be, they all agree that there is something seriously wrong with the present-day sermon. Some even question the whole phenomenon of preaching and go so far as to suggest that in our modern age the church should give up preaching altogether and look for other, more suitable, forms of communication. But the scholars and experts are not the only ones who complain. More serious is the dissatisfaction among those who still attend the church services. The church may claim that its message is the most exciting message that has ever been proclaimed, but what people in reality hear is often little else than – to use the phrase of G. Ebeling – "institutionally assured platitudes".

It is evident that this kind of criticism touches the very heart of our preaching activity. It is also evident that we cannot ignore it and proceed to the order of the (Sun)day. Nevertheless, it would be no better to give in to it and embark on all kinds of wild experiments. I believe we have to do two things. On the one hand, we have to take these criticisms seriously. On the other hand, we have to submit them to the test of God's Word. This is the reason why we are now posing the fundamental question: "What really is preaching?" Only when we find the answer to this question can we attain to a true renewal of preaching. Renewal is not a matter of all kinds of gimmicks. It is not even a matter of better methods, however important they may be. At this point I fully agree with the Roman Catholic theologian, Jerome Murphy-O'Connor, when he writes: "The experience of the lay apostolate and the liturgical movement has shown that a renewal on the level of technique alone is not really a renewal at all, and in practice neither effective nor lasting. True renewal must begin with a profound appreciation of the nature of preaching, a realization of just what preaching is".[1]

☆   ☆   ☆

To find the answer to our question we have primarily to return to the *New Testament*, for there we find the origin of Christian preaching. We may even go a step further and say:the New Testament itself is both the result of Christian preaching and also a form of Christian preaching. The Gospels, for instance, were not written out of a merely historical and/or biographical interest in the person of the so-called historical Jesus, but the authors, being members of the Christian church, summarized in their Gospel the preaching of their church concerning the Lord who died on the cross and who arose again on the third day. In a detailed study of *The Apostolic Preaching and Its Developments*,[2] C.H. Dodd wrote concerning the Gospel of Mark that the evangelist "conceived himself as writing a form of *kerygma*".[3] The same is true of Matthew and Luke, even though at times "the emphases are different".[4]Dodd's own conclusion is that "the fourfold Gospel taken as a whole is an expression of the original apostolic preaching".[5] He also points out that the early church was aware of this. The Muratorian Canon, probably representing the work of Hippolytus, the dissent-

---

[1]Jermone Murphy-O'Connor, *Paul on Preaching*, 1964, XIV,XV. Cf. also Domino Grasso S. J., *Proclaiming God's Message. A Study in the Theology of Preaching*, 1965, XVII.
[2]C.H. Dodd, *The Apostolic Preaching and Its Developments*, 1st edition 1936.
[3]*Op. cit.*, 1963, 47.
[4]*Op. cit.*, 52.
[5]*Op. cit.*, 55.

ing bishop of Rome about the end of the second century, clearly states that the four Gospels embody the original apostolic preaching of the "saving facts".[6]

How central preaching was to the life of the early church appears also from the fact that the New Testament has no fewer than thirty different verbs for preaching. G. Friedrich, who mentions them all in his article on 'keryssein' in the *Theological Dictionary of the New Testament*,[7] rightly points out that our almost exclusive use of 'preaching'[8] for all of them is a sign not merely of poverty of vocabulary, but also of the loss of something that was a living reality in primitive Christianity. How much of a living reality it was we can read on almost every page of the New Testament. The new movement was from the very beginning a *preaching movement*. It all started with the preaching activity of John the Baptist, the forerunner and herald of the coming Messiah. Jesus' own ministry is basically a preaching ministry too. Mark describes it as follows: "Now after John was arrested, Jesus came into Galilee, preaching the gospel of God, and saying: 'The time is fulfilled, and the Kingdom of God is at hand; repent, and believe in the gospel'" (Mark 1:14,15). To be sure, Jesus' preaching was accompanied by mighty signs and wonders, but these were not an entirely different aspect of his ministry. Rather they underscored his proclamation that the Kingdom was at hand; even more, they showed that in him and in his preaching the Kingdom was already becoming manifest.

When Jesus himself appoints the twelve, he gives them the same task: "to preach and have authority to cast out demons" (Mark 3:14, 15). Later on we read that the twelve

---

[6]*Op.cit.,* 55. The quotation from the Muratorian Canon reads: "Although various principles are taught in the several Gospel-books, this makes no difference to the faith of believers, since by one governing Spirit in them all, the facts are declared concerning the Nativity, the Passion, the Resurrection, His converse with the disciples, and His two advents, the first which was in humility of aspect, according to the power of His royal Father, and the glorious one which is yet to come."

[7]*Theological Dictionary of the New Testment (TDNT),* III, 703.

[8]The Latin verb 'praedicare', from which our word 'to preach' has been derived, has only two meanings: 1) to make publicly known, proclaim, publish; 2) to praise, commend, eulogize, boast. These meanings do not nearly express the richness of the biblical concept of preaching.

are actually sent out on a preaching mission (Mark 6:7–13; Matt. 10:5–42)[9], while Luke tells us of a similar mission of seventy disciples (Luke 10:1–16). After the resurrection the commission to preach the gospel is repeated. How important this commission was to the primitive church appears from the fact that it is mentioned at the close of all four Gospels (Matt. 28:19, 20; Mark 16:15; Luke 24:47, 48; John 20:21) and also at the beginning of the Book of Acts (Acts 1:8). In Acts we also see how immediately after the outpouring of the Holy Spirit on the day of Pentecost the new Christian church becomes a preaching church. Peter arises and proclaims the crucified but risen Jesus as both Lord and Messiah (2:36). And so it goes on throughout the whole Book of Acts. At first Peter is the prominent preacher, but we should not forget that there were others as well, e.g. Stephen and Philip. Indeed, when after the martyrdom of Stephen the congregation is scattered by persecution, we read that "those who were scattered went about preaching the word" (8:4). In the second half of Acts Paul replaces Peter as the foremost preacher, but again he is only one of the many. The entire early church is a preaching church. It is therefore not surprising that the documents of this church, in so far as they have been preserved in the New Testament, are full of preaching material. Indeed, it can even be said that all these documents, each in its own way, are themselves preaching material. It is no exaggeration if one says of the whole Christian movement: "In the beginning was the Sermon".[10]

✻   ✻   ✻

But there is still more to be said. However much it is true that preaching is a specifically Christian activity, it is not something altogether new. It has its roots in the *Old Testa-*

---

[9]In Mark 6:12, 13 we again find the combination of preaching and casting out demons.

[10]Thus E. Fascher summarized the formcritical approach of Martin Dibelius. Cf. E. Fascher, *Die formgeschichtliche Methode*, 1924, 54.

ment. It may safely be said that the religion of Israel was a *prophetic religion* or, if you wish, a *religion of the word*. At first glance this may seem to be a rather one-sided statement, to say the least. Is it not characteristic of the God of Israel that he is a God who *acts* in the history of his people (and of the whole world)?[11] Is it therefore not more apt to speak of his revelation as a revelation in the events of history, rather than as a word-revelation? It cannot .be denied, of course, that the Old Testament often speaks of God's acts in the history of his people. And yet we wish to maintain that basically God's self-revelation is a word-revelation.

1. The most common and most fundamental revelatory act Scripture attributes to God is his *speaking*. It is through his sovereign speaking that heaven and earth were created. The author of Genesis 1 says it in majestic simplicity: "And God said: 'Let there be light', and there was light" (Gn. 1:3), and the author of Psalm 33 calls all inhabitants of the earth to stand in awe of him, "for he spoke and it came to be, he commanded, and it came forth" (33:8, 9). In the story of redemption the situation is not different. The story of Israel begins with the call of Abraham by God and with the promises God gives him. The special relationship of Israel as a nation "rests from the first on the word of this God. The basic law of the Sinai covenant, the Decalogue, is given the name 'the ten words'"[12] (cf. Deut. 4:13; 10:4). And "side by side with this divine word in the law, with its validity for all occasions, we find the particular proclamation of the divine will for particular situations, the prophetic word of God".[13]

2. But even when God acts in history, his activity *never* takes place *without the revealing word*. This is not surprising, for all that happens in history shares in the ambiguity of all history and is subject to many, often contradictory interpretations. Therefore God always makes his purpose known before hand, so that his people may know that it is he who acts. When God decides to lead his people out of the house

---

[11]Cf. G. Ernest Wright and Reginald H. Fuller, *The Book of the Acts of God. Contemporary scholarship interprets the Bible*, 1960.
[12]Walther Eichrodt, *Theology of the Old Testament*, Vol. II, 1967, 71.
[13]*Op. cit.*, 72.

of bondage in Egypt, he first reveals himself to Moses at the burning bush and informs him that he will redeem his people (Ex. 3:7–10). Th.C. Vriezen points out that this is not an exception. On the contrary, over against G. von Rad he maintains that "the Old Testament itself always lets God's action in history be preceded by the prophetic word. According to the unanimous verdict of all Old Testament witnesses, the prophetic word does not come as an *a posteriori* interpretation, but it always ushers in the event. Both the prophetic word and its realization in history have as their purpose the restoration of the relation of the people to God, who is the God of Israel".[14]

3. Thirdly, we notice in the Old Testament that the story of God's revealing and redeeming activity in the history of his people has to be *passed on*, by word of mouth, from generation to generation. In the Mosaic law we find several references (e.g., Ex. 13:8, 14; Deut. 6:21). Very clearly and beautifully it is put in the opening verses of Psalm 78:

> Give ear, O my people, to my teaching;
> incline your ears to the words of my mouth!
> I will open my mouth in a parable;
> I will utter dark sayings from of old,
> things that we have heard and known,
> that our fathers have told us.
> We will not hide them from their children,
> but tell to the coming generation
> the glorious deeds of the Lord, and his might,
> and the wonders which he has wrought.
>
> (Ps. 78:1–4)

In the prophetic literature an even wider perspective is

---

[14]Th. C. Vriezen, 'Geloof, Openbaring en Geschiedenis' (Faith, Revelation and History), two articles in *Kerk en Theologie*, XVI(1965), 97ff. and 210ff. The quotation is taken from p.215 Cf. also the following words on p.216:"It is not true that God reveals Himself in history in a shadowy way, but God is recognized in history in the way He had revealed Himself to the prophets, and history confirms his word". Cf. also J.I. Packer in the article on 'Revelation' in the *New Bible Dictionary*, 1962, 1093: "The thought of God as revealed in His actions is secondary, and depends for its validity on the presupposition of verbal revelation. For men can only 'know that He is Yahweh' from seeing His works in history if He speaks to make it clear that they are His works, and to explain what they mean. Equally, men could never have guessed of deduced who and what Jesus of Nazareth was apart from God's statements about Him in the Old Testament, and Jesus' own self-testimony."

opened. There will come a future, in which not only the children of Israel but all nations will share in the redemptive activities of this God (cf. Is. 2:1–4; 25:6–9; 60; Jer. 3:17; Micah 4:1–4; Zech. 8:20ff.; cf. also the sayings about the Servant of the Lord, Is. 42:4; 49:6; 52:13–15).

☆   ☆   ☆

This future has been inaugurated on the day of Pentecost, when the Spirit comes and breaks down the barriers between Israel and the 'goyim', the heathen nations. Now it becomes true what Joel already had foretold; "It shall be that whoever calls on the name of the Lord shall be saved" (Acts 2:21; cf. Joel 2:32). "Whoever" – there is no distinction any more. "Whoever calls on the name of the Lord" – be he Jew or Gentile. But this calling upon the name of the Lord presupposes the preaching of this Name. As Paul puts it so clearly in Rom. 10:14, 15: "But how are men to call upon him in whom they have not believed? And how are they to believe in him whom they have never heard? And how are they to hear without a preacher? And how can men preach unless they are sent? As it is written: 'How beautiful are the feet of those who preach good news!'".

Preaching is as necessary for the Christian faith as breathing is for the life of man. Without the preaching of the gospel there is no faith. For this reason the New Testament does not make any difference in principle between missionary and congregational preaching, between preaching *extra muros* and *intra muros*. Today it is generally recognized that the fundamental distinction which C.H. Dodd made between *kerygma* (i.e. missionary preaching) and *didache* (i.e. congregational preaching) is not tenable.[15] In the New Testament the terms are often used together and even interchangeably. What is more, the content of both terms is

---

[15]Cf. C.H. Dodd, *op. cit.*, 7 and passim. For an extensive discussion of Dodd's view, see Robert C. Worley, *Preaching and Teaching in the Earliest Church*, 1967, and James I.H. McDonald, *Kerygma and Didache*, Society for New Testament Studies Monograph Series, no. 37.

essentially the same.[16] This is not to deny that there are different emphases. In missionary preaching the *kerygma* will be in the foreground, but it will always naturally issue in *didache*, for the outsider who accepts the message of the *kerygma* will also need instruction about its meaning and consequences. In congregational preaching the emphasis will be upon the *unfolding* of the message of the *kerygma*, showing all its implications for faith and life. But the congregation also constantly needs to hear the *kerygma* itself. The message of salvation is not like a film one has to see only once or a novel one has to read only once, and from then onwards one knows the 'plot'. No, the Christian congregation too has to hear the message again and again. There is no Sunday in our life on which we need not hear the joyful message of the Father who is waiting for his wandering son or daughter.

✧   ✧   ✧

But we have to delve still deeper into the New Testament. It not only shows us that Christian preaching is indispensable for both the congregation and the world, but it also tells us what the deepest *nature* of preaching is. Admittedly, the New Testament does not contain a special treatise on the essence of preaching. The reason why the early church did not feel the need for such a treatise may simply have been that they all were far too busy doing it and saw so very clearly that the Lord blessed their efforts. Yet there are enough indications in the New Testament to discover what it regards as the essential nature of preaching.

1. First, there are the many *terms* used for preaching. This is not the place for an extended discussion. The interested reader may refer to the 1978 *Tyndale Bulletin*, where I discuss six key terms.[17] I quote from my summary of results.[18] First of

---

[16]Cf. my article, 'What is preaching according to the New Testament?', in *Tyndale Bulletin*, 29(1978), 14ff.

[17]*Op. cit.*, 7–19.

[18]*Op. cit.*, 18,19.

all, it appears from the use of the term *keryssein* (=to proclaim) that preaching is not only the proclamation of a saving event that once took place, some twenty centuries ago, in the life, death and resurrection of Jesus Christ, but that the proclamation of this event also inaugurates the new state of affairs for the believing listener. When he believes in Jesus Christ as the Saviour, he at the very same time participates in the salvation brought about by him. The verb *euangelizesthai*, which is virtually synonymous with *keryssein*, underscores that the message about Jesus Christ is a joyful message. The verb *martyrein* (= to witness), in so far as it is applicable to present-day preaching, indicates that all true preaching has to adhere to the apostolic tradition. *Didaskein* (= to teach) emphasizes that the preacher also has to unfold the message as to its meaning and consequences, both dogmatically and ethically. Finally, *propheteuein* (= to prophesy) and *parakalein* (= to comfort, admonish) tell us that the message may not remain an abstraction but has to be applied to the concrete situation of the listeners.

To sum it all up, the various terms used in the New Testament show that Christian preaching is more than just recounting the story *about* the Word of God spoken in Jesus Christ. In Christian preaching *this Word itself* comes to the listeners. Indeed, we must go even further and say that Christian preaching *is* the Word of God coming to men. As G. Friedrich says: "The Word proclaimed is a divine Word, and as such it is an effective force which creates what it proclaims. Hence preaching is no mere impartation of facts. It is an event. What is proclaimed takes place."[19]

✳   ✳   ✳

2. This conclusion is confirmed by a second line of investigation. The New Testament may not contain an explicit exposition of what preaching is, yet there are many scattered references that throw light on the question under discussion.

[19]*TDNT*, III, 709.

As far as the *Gospels* are concerned, it must suffice to point out two things. First of all, we notice that *Jesus identifies himself with the "messenger of good news" in Second-Isaiah.* This gives a very special quality to his preaching. He does not preach the Gospel of the Kingdom as referring to a merely eschatological entity, but he preaches it as an existent reality. In his preaching the salvation of the Kingdom is already present. Herman Ridderbos puts it thus: "His preaching is not only characterized as prophecy and announcement, but also as proclamation and promulgation".[20] His words are a manifestation of the creative Word of God that does not return empty but accomplishes that which he purposes and prospers in the thing for which he sends it (Is. 55:11). Secondly, we notice that *Jesus also identifies himself with the apostles in their mission.* They are his representatives, in whose preaching he himself comes to the people. Yes, Jesus even includes God in this identification, which can only mean that the words of the apostles also share in the creativity of the divine Word. In Luke 10:16 Jesus says it quite openly and plainly to the seventy who are sent on a special preaching mission: "He who hears you hears me, and he who rejects you rejects me, and he who rejects me rejects him who sent me" (cf. also Matt. 10:40). After the resurrection this promise of identification is repeated in several ways. When in Matthew 28 Jesus issues the Great Commission, he adds the promise that he will be with them "always, to the close of the age" (28:20). In the Gospel of John it is stated even more explicitly. "As the Father sent me, even so I send you" (20:21). Then Jesus breathes on them and says: "Receive the Holy Spirit. If you forgive the sins of any, they are forgiven; if you retain the sins of any, they are retained" (20:22). Here the identification is complete. In the apostolic preaching of the gospel the keys of the Kingdom function: the Kingdom is opened to believers and shut against unbelievers.[21]

[20]Herman Ridderbos, *The Coming of the Kingdom,* 1962, 73.
[21]Cf. Heidelberg Catechism (1563), Lord's Day XXXI, where we read in Question and Answer 84: "How is the kingdom of heaven opened and shut by the preaching of the holy gospel? In this way: The kingdom of heaven is opened when it is proclaimed and openly testified to believers, one and all, according to the command of Christ, that as often as they accept the promise of the gospel with true

We find the same identification between the preached word and the Word of God in the *letters of St, Paul*. Time and again he describes the message he brings as "the Word of God", or "the Word of the Lord", or simply "the Word" (1 Thess. 1:6, 8; 2 Thess. 3:1; Col. 1:25; 4:3; cf. also 2 Tim. 2:9; 4:1; 1 Pet. 1:23f.; Heb. 4:12f.). These expressions are not just figures of speech that should not be taken too literally. On the contrary, Paul uses the term "Word" or "Word of God" also for the written word of the Old Testament (cf. Rom. 6:6, 9; 1 Cor. 15:54; Gal. 5:14), and there can be no doubt that in all these passages "God Himself is firmly regarded as the One who speaks in Scripture".[22] By using the same terminology for his own preaching the apostle obviously claims that God is also the real Subject of this preaching and that it carries the same authority as the Old Testament Scriptures. How much Paul is in earnest about this becomes abundantly clear when he writes to the Thessalonians: "We also thank God constantly for this, that when you received the Word of God, which you heard from us [= the preached word!], you accepted it not as the word of men, but as what it really is, the Word of God, which is at work in you believers" (1 Thess. 2:13). It could not be more emphatically stated that the apostolic preaching is not of man's devising, but has its origin in God and, therefore, is in very truth God's own Word. It is not partly human and partly divine, whereby it is left to the Thessalonians to determine which parts are human and which divine (the liberal view); nor is it a human word that, where and when it pleases God, may *become* the Word of God (the Barthian view). No, its real essence is that God himself speaks in and through the words of his servants.[23]

This also explains why the Word preached by Paul and his fellow-workers is *effective*. This efficacy is not due to the

faith all their sins are truly forgiven them by God for the sake of Christ's gracious work. On the contrary, the wrath of God and eternal condemnation fall upon all unbelievers and hypocrites as long as they do not repent. It is according to this witness of the gospel that God will judge the one and the other in this life and in the life to come." Cf. *Reformed Confessions of the Sixteenth Century*, ed. by Arthur Cochrane, 1966, 321.

[22]*TDNT*, IV, 111.

[23]For more details, see my *Tyndale Bulletin* article cited in n.16 above, 25ff.

qualities of the preacher, however important such qualities may be (cf. 1 Thess. 2:10 and the first chapter of 2 Corinthians). The efficacy is wholly due to him whose Word it is. The secret lies in the genitive: it is the Word of *God*. This is not a genitive of object (= it is a word *about* God), but of subject: God is the real Speaker. Therefore the author of Hebrews can write: "The Word of God is living and active (full of energy!), sharper than any two-edged sword, piercing to the division of soul and spirit, of joints and marrow, and discerning the thoughts and intentions of the heart" (4:12). Or as Paul himself puts it: "The gospel is a *power of God* [again the genitive of subject] for salvation to every one who has faith" (Rom. 1:16; cf. 1 Cor. 1:18). All these passages reveal the same basic idea: that of identification. The word preached by the apostles and the Word of God cannot be separated.

✧   ✧   ✧

But – and this is a very essential question – does this also apply to *our preaching today*? Is not Paul's position (and the same applies to the other apostles) so *unique* that we cannot possibly equate ourselves and our preaching with the apostle and his preaching? Dare we say of our own preaching: it is really the Word of God? And even apart from daring, may we make this claim on behalf of our preaching today?

We must begin with acknowledging the *uniqueness of the apostolate*. These men, who were the witnesses of the resurrection, were commissioned by the risen Lord himself. Already before his death he had given them the special promise of the Holy Spirit as the Paraclete, the Helper and Counsellor, and after the resurrection this promise was fulfilled (cf. John 20:21–23; Acts 2:1ff. compared with 1:8). This is also the reason why these men have a very special, even unique position in the early church. They, with their preaching, are not an accidental appendage to the divine revelation in Jesus Christ, but as Herman Ridderbos puts it: their "preaching of redemption, as apostolic preaching, belongs to the actuality of revelation and as such it has its own unique character".[24] These men are instruments of revelation and as such they are the foundation of the church. In all subsequent ages the church is bound to their preaching as the final norm of faith.[25]

It is quite obvious that in *this* respect our preaching can never be equated with that of the apostles. We are not in the same way instruments of revelation. We did not, like Paul, receive the Gospel by special revelation (cf. Gal. 1:11, 12, 15, 16). We received the Gospel from those who came before us. Our knowledge of God is never first-hand but always second-hand. These are essential differences between the apostles and present-day preachers. However, that does not mean that therefore our preaching is only a human word and not God's Word. It is striking that at *this* point Paul never differentiates between his own preaching and that of his fellow-workers. When he writes to his congregations about Timothy (1 Thess. 3:2, 3; 1 Cor. 16:10) or when he writes to Timothy himself (2 Tim. 2:2; 4:2), he uses the same terms which he used for his own preaching. What is more, in 2 Tim. 2:2 Timothy is charged to commit to others what he has heard. They must be "faithful men, who shall be able to teach [*didaskein!*] others also". In other words, they are teachers (and preachers) at third hand! But it does not make any real difference, as long as they preach the gospel they heard from Timothy, who in turn had heard it from Paul. It is one chain of tradition and every "faithful" link has the same divine power as the first and basic link (cf. also 2 Tim. 1:14 and 1 Tim. 5:17; 6:20).

On the basis of all these data we can only conclude that in the New Testament preaching is much more than the communication of facts. To be true, preaching has a factual content (cf. Rom. 1:1, 3; 1 Cor. 15:1ff.; etc.). But preaching itself is much more than a cognitive communication. In the act of preaching the saving power of these facts becomes a present reality for the hearer. True preaching is an event. Paul calls the gospel a *"power* unto salvation" (Rom. 1:16). When the gospel is preached, something *happens*. In the next verse Paul describes this 'something' as follows: "In it

[24]H.N. Ridderbos, *The Authority of the New Testament Scriptures*, 1963, 17.
[25]Cf. H.N. Ridderbos, *op. cit.*, 14, 15.

(= the gospel) the righteousness of God is being revealed through faith for faith" (1:17). We should note that Paul uses the verb 'to reveal' and that he uses it in the present tense. The righteousness of God is not just *described* in the preached Gospel, it is not even primarily *offered*, but it is *revealed*. It is un-veiled as a present reality. Or as John Murray puts it: "In the Gospel the righteousness of God is actively and dynamically brought to bear upon man's sinful situation ... It is redemptively active in the sphere of human sin and ruin."[26] Preaching this Gospel, therefore, is a very dynamic happening. It is not to be compared with a prospectus that is sent through the mail, after which one can order the items offered, but it is rather like a love-letter, in which love itself shines through in such a way that the reader feels it as a present reality. In the letter the writer himself, as it were, comes along. But in the preaching of the Gospel it is still deeper and richer, for here we have to do with the risen Lord who not only sends a message, but who, in the *modus* of the Holy Spirit, personally comes along with the message. Heinrich Schlier rightly says: "Christ is present in the Word and meets the hearer. And the same is true of all those realities which are indicated by genitives ... The cross arises before my eyes in the 'word of the cross'; reconciliation happens in the 'word of reconciliation'; glory shines forth in the 'word of glory'; life and immortality make their appearance, etc. And this, too, happens in the power of the Holy Spirit, who acts as the Revealer in this word".[27]

✣   ✣   ✣

When we now go beyond the New Testament and immediately move on to the *theology of the Reformers*, we do not mean to say that there has not been any proper view of preaching between the New Testament and the Reformation. Many church fathers had a very high view of preaching. We need only to mention the names of Chrysos-

[26]John Murray, *The Epistle of Paul to the Romans*, Vol. I, 1960, 29, 30.
[27]Heinrich Schlier, *Het Woord Gods*, 1959, 68. Original German title: *Wort Gottes*.

tom and Augustine. The reason why we immediately proceed to the Reformers is rather that in their theology of preaching they rediscovered the teaching of the New Testament itself. Again preaching became the means of grace *par excellence*.

When *Luther* rediscovered that the Pauline doctrine of justification means a declaratory act of God, by which he justifies the sinner "by grace, for Christ's sake, through faith"[28], the sermon was bound to become the very centre of the worship service. For it is in the preaching of the gospel that this declaration is made. For Luther preaching was a very *dynamic* event. Indeed, it was an *apocalyptic* event,[29] in which the battle with the great adversary was fought once again. "Every sermon for him was a struggle for souls. Eternal issues were being settled in the moment of preaching – the issues of life and death, light and darkness, sin and grace, the kingdom of Christ and the kingdom of Satan."[30] But above all it was a *saving* event. In the preaching of the gospel Jesus Christ himself comes to us with all his salvation. Every one who listens to this Gospel in faith is being saved at that very moment. No wonder that Luther has no difficulty whatever in calling the preacher himself the "mouth-piece of God". "God", he declares, "the Creator of heaven and earth, speaks with you through his preachers, baptizes, catechizes, absolves you through the ministry of his own sacraments. These are the words of God, not of Plato or Aristotle. It is God Himself who speaks".[31]

Calvin had an equally high view of preaching. For him, too, the preachers are mouthpieces of God.[32] He, too, regards preaching itself as a living, apocalyptic, saving event. He

[28]*Confession of Augsburg* (1930), Art. IV.
[29]Cf. A. Niebergall, 'Die Geschichte der christlichen Predigt', in *Leitourgia*, II, 261f.
[30]A. Skevington Wood, *Captive to the Word. Martin Luther, Doctor of Sacred Scripture*, 1969, 91.
[31]W.A., *Tischreden*, 4. 531. No. 4812. Cf. Skevington Wood, *op. cit.*, 93.
[32]J. Calvin, Homilies on I Sam. 42, CR, XXXIX, 705. Dealing with the jurisdiction of the church, he writes in his *Institutes* "that the word of the Gospel, whatever man may preach it, is the very sentence of God, published at the supreme judgment seat, written in the book of life, ratified firm and fixed, in heaven" (IV,xi, 1). Cf. for a whole series of quotations from Calvin's works, T.H.L. Parker, *The Oracles of God. An Introduction to the Preaching of John Calvin*, 1947, 54ff.

does not hesitate to say that "when the Gospel is preached, Christ's blood distils together with the voice."[33]
How much the Reformation was in earnest about all this appears from the fact that they inserted statements about preaching in their *confessions*. Immediately after the article on Justification (art. IV) the *Augsburg Confession* (1530) speaks of The office of the Ministry (art. V). "To obtain such faith God instituted the office of the ministry, that is, provided the Gospel and the sacraments. Through these as through means, He gives the Holy Spirit, who works faith where and when He pleases, in those who hear the Gospel." The most important confessional statement is found in the first chapter of the *Second Helvetic Confession (Confessio Helvetica Posterior)* (1566), written by Heinrich Bullinger, the successor of Zwingli. The chapter opens with the confession that the canonical Scriptures are the "true Word of God". "God Himself spoke to the fathers, prophets and apostles, and still speaks to us through the Holy Scriptures". Further on in the same chapter Bullinger also speaks of preaching and states very succinctly but also very incisively: "The preaching of the Word of God is the Word of God" (*Praedicatio verbi Dei est verbum Dei*).[34] The copula 'is' (*est*) clearly indicates identity. That this was indeed Bullinger's intention appears from what immediately follows: "Wherefore, when this Word of God (= Scripture) is now preached in the church by preachers lawfully called, we believe that the *very Word of God* is proclaimed and received by the faithful." Here we have the high view of preaching, as it is held by the whole Reformation, in a nutshell. Of course, we should bear in mind that such statements are not meant as definitions, based on a careful, empirical analysis of a great number of sermons. The Reformers never meant by such statements that every sermon is *de facto* the Word of God. Such statements are *confessions of faith*! They issue from the firm belief, based on Scripture itself, that wherever the gospel is faithfully preached, God himself is involved and present with his saving grace. We should never forget that in the Helvetic Confession Bullinger's phrase: "The preaching of

[33]John Calvin, *Commentary* on Heb. 9:21 and 10:19.
[34]Cf. Arthur Cochrane, *op. cit.*, 224.

the Word of God is the Word of God", is preceded by Jesus' own promise: "He who hears you hears me, and he who rejects me rejects him who sent me (Matt. 10:40; Luke 10:16; John 13:20)."[35] This is the deepest secret of all true preaching.

☆ ☆ ☆

In the orthodox Reformation tradition this same high view has always been retained. In nearly all homiletical and also many dogmatical works, representing this tradition, the famous statement of Bullinger is mentioned with approval and concurrence. In our century this high view of the Reformation has been vigorously defended again by *Karl Barth*.[36] In strong reaction against the older liberal theology, which had virtually lost every idea of revelation as the self-revelation of God by God himself and had replaced it by man's discovery of God, Barth maintained that from beginning to end revelation is God's own work. Yes, revelation is a fully trinitarian activity: the Father reveals himself in the Son through the Holy Spirit. The triune God is Revealer, Revelation and Revealedness. In all eternity God decided to reveal himself to man in his Son Jesus Christ. In time God the Son executed this revelation in his own person and work in that he assumed human nature and became man as Jesus of Nazareth. God the Holy Spirit consummates this revelation by opening man's heart, so that man is capable of receiving the revelation and actually does receive it.[37] From this it follows that for Barth Jesus Christ is the Word of God *par excellence*. In him there is a *direct identity* with the Word of God. But he is not the only Word of God. In line with the whole Reformation tradition Barth distinguishes a threefold Word of God: Jesus Christ as the incarnate Son of God is the

[35]*Op. cit.*, 224/5.

[36]Cf. my article on 'Barth's View of Preaching', in *Vox Reformata* (published by the Faculty of the Reformed Theological College, Geelong, Vic., Australia), No. 33 (1979), 12–21.

[37]Cf. Karl Barth, *Church Dogmatics (CD)*, I, 1, 339ff.; I, 2, 203ff. Cf. also Herbert Hartwell, *The Theology of Karl Barth: an Introduction*, 1964, 67ff.

first form of the Word of God; the revealed Word; Scripture as the witness to Jesus Christ by prophets and apostles is the second form of the Word of God: the written Word; finally, preaching, which is the church's proclamation of the prophetic and apostolic witness to Jesus Christ, is the third form: the preached Word.[38] To be true, the second form (Scripture) is not on a par with the first (God's Word in Jesus Christ), and the third (preaching) is not on a a par with the second. In the case of both the second and the third form we may not speak of direct identity with the Word of God, but only of an *indirect identity*. Both Scripture and preaching, by themselves, are no more than fallible human witnesses to the Word of God in Jesus Christ. Yet, *where and when it pleases God*, they may *become* the Word of God and at that very moment they *are* the Word of God for the reader or listener.[39]

From these few remarks it is clear that Barth too has a very high view of preaching. In this view there is also place for the *'est'* of the Second Helvetic Confession. As a matter of fact, Barth himself quotes the famous statement: *"Praedicatio verbi Dei est verbum Dei"*, with approval,[40] and to my mind rightly so. Both Bullinger and Barth agree that God *has* revealed himself in Jesus Christ and that both the Old and the New Testament bear witness to this revelation. They also agree that true preaching is the proclamation of this witness of Scripture. But at this very point their ways part. Bullinger – in full agreement with all the other Reformers – believes that Scripture *is* the Word of God and that preaching, when it is the faithful proclamation of Scripture, *is* also the Word of God. For Barth they must first *become* the Word of God, through an act of God, before they can *be* the Word of God. But even so, compared with the older liberal and also many neo-liberal views, Barth's view is very high indeed. It is a view of preaching in which Scripture occupies the central place. In fact, Barth never tired of reiterating that the only task of the preacher is to witness to Jesus Christ as the revealing and reconciling Word of God, and to do this by

[38]Cf. *CD*, I, 1, 98ff.
[39]Cf. my book *Karl Barth's Doctrine of Holy Scripture*, 1962, 116ff.
[40]*CD*, I, 1, 56.

interpreting the prophetic and apostolic witness to this Word. That's all there is to it. The preacher need not worry about the question of whether his preaching will bring the message 'home' to the listeners. He may leave that safely to God. All the preacher himself has to do is to *repeat* (German: *nachsagen*) the biblical witness in his own words. That, in a nutshell, is Barth's whole theory of preaching. I think we must say that in many ways it is a beautiful theory. Its beauty lies not only in the fact that it gives all glory to God alone, but also in its simplicity. *All* the preacher has to do is to repeat the message of Scripture in his own words.

But – is this really all? After World War II many *young theologians in Germany* were of the opinion that Barth's theory was one-sided. To be sure, they would agree with him that revelation is always an act of God, also in preaching. They would also agree with him that the message to be proclaimed is found in Scripture, which is the witness to God's revelation in Jesus Christ. Dogmatically this is entirely true. But, they asked, is it also homiletically true? Is preaching not more than just repeating the message of Scripture in one's own words? Does the preacher not have to deal with two 'factors': the message of Scripture, on the one hand, and the life of his listeners, on the other? Is preaching not like an *ellipse* instead of a circle? A circle has only one centre, an ellipse has two foci. Are there not two foci in preaching: Scripture and the listener? I think this critique was basically justified (even though, as I hope to show in Chapter Four, I do not agree with the solution offered by the critics). Preaching is not a simple one-way movement from Scripture to the listener. I believe it is more complex than that. Preaching is a meeting, an encounter of the Word of God in Scripture with the people in their concrete, historical situation. And preparing and delivering a sermon means that these two foci have to be interrelated in a process of continual reciprocity. I believe that this interrelating of Scripture and the situation of the listener may also be the answer to many of the criticisms which I mentioned in the first chapter. In fact, the remaining chapters will gravitate around this problem.

THREE

Preaching and the Bible

We begin with the thesis that if our preaching is to be *Christian* preaching, it has to be *biblical* preaching. Such a thesis almost sounds like a truism. And yet this is most certainly not so, for there have been many periods in the history of the Christian church in which preaching was far from biblical. In the Middle Ages, for instance, preaching was often a moralizing tale rather than a biblical exposition. The Reformation of the sixteenth century changed this and put preaching back on a squarely biblical basis. The famous statement of the *Second Helvetic Confession* not only says that the preaching of the Word of God *is* the Word of God, but also indicates what it means by "the preaching of the Word of God". For in the next sentence this is interpreted as follows: "When *this Word of God* (= Scripture) is preached in the church by preachers lawfully called, we believe that the very Word of God is proclaimed, and received by the faithful" (chapter I). A few years earlier the Reformed Church of France had already stated in its first *Liturgy*: "For the message of salvation, the minister in his preaching will take some text in Holy Scripture and read it fully, as Jesus did in Nazareth. After the reading, he will speak, not desultorily, but on the passage read, introducing passages which are in Scripture and which are useful in the exposition of Scripture, which he will explain without departing from Holy Scripture. This he will do in order not to mix the pure Word of God with the refuse of men, faithfully communicating the Word and speaking the Word of God only."[1] Likewise the *Thirty-Nine Articles* state in art. XIX (which is clearly based on art. VII of the *Augsburg Confession*): "The visible Church of Christ is a congregation of faithful men, in the which the pure Word of God is preached", and it is further evident from the articles VI and XX that this pure Word of God is to be the Word which we find in Holy Scripture.

Fortunately, this has always remained the fundamental view in the tradition of the Reformation, both on the European continent and in the Anglo-Saxon world. In my own Dutch Reformed tradition the great work on *Reformed Homiletics* by one of my predecessors in the seminary at Kampen, T. Hoekstra, reiterated again and again:"Preaching is the exposition and application of Holy Scripture."[2] Karl Barth, who stood in the Swiss Reformed tradition, also never tired of emphasizing this same point. For the evangelical Anglican tradition I would like to quote Dr. D.B. Knox, Principal of Moore College, Sydney: "This is what preaching should consist in – exposition of the teaching of Scripture and application to life's situation."[3] And I am glad to say that one of the modern confessions in the Reformed/Presbyterian tradition, *The Confession of 1967*, is also very clear on this point: "God's word is spoken to his church today where the Scriptures are faithfully preached and attentively read in dependence on the illumination of the Holy Spirit and with readiness to receive their truth and direction" (9.30).

This emphasiss on Christian preaching as biblical preaching is in full conformity with Scripture itself. When Paul writes to Timothy about the 'sacred writings', he adds:

[1]Quoted from Pierre Ch. Marcel, *The Relevance of Preaching*, 1963, 58/59.

[2]T. Hoekstra, *Gereformeerde Prediking* (1962), 157, 160, 161, 162, 163.

[3]David Broughton Knox, *Thirty-Nine Articles*, 1967, 24. Cf. also E.A. Litton, *Introduction to Dogmatic Theology*, 1960, 430: "To us who live in these latter times, the inspired volume is the only authentic source of what the preacher has to deliver.....The preacher, therefore, ought to be, above all things, an expositor of Scripture." In *Knots Untied* Bishop J.C. Ryle writes: "In complete public worship there should be the *preaching of God's Word*. I can find no record of Church assemblies in the New Testament in which preaching and teaching orally does not occupy a most prominent position. It appears to me to be the chief instrument by which the Holy Ghost not only awakens sinners, but also leads on and establishes saints", 1959, 197.

"which are able to instruct you for salvation through faith in Jesus Christ". And then there follows the well-known statement about the inspiration and purpose of Scripture: "All Scripture is inspired by God and profitable for teaching, for reproof, for correction, and for training in righteousness, that the man of God may be complete, equipped for every good work" (2 Tim. 3:15–17). Actually, this description of the purpose of the Bible is an equally valid description of the purpose of preaching. For that is what preaching is for: teaching, reproof, correction, training in righteousness. We may go a step further and say that the Scriptures, having such a purpose, are themselves documents of preaching. This has been generally recognized in our century. In his famous lectures, quoted above, Forsyth put it thus: "The great reason why the preacher must return continually to the Bible is that the Bible is the greatest sermon in the world. Above every other function of it the Bible is a sermon, a *kerygma*, a preachment. It is the preacher's book because it is the preaching book."[4] In it we hear the voices of prophets and apostles proclaiming to the people of their own time the great acts of God in the history of Israel and in the life, death and resurrection of Jesus Christ, who as the Son of God incarnate is the true son of Israel. And these prophets and apostles invite the church of today to continue this proclamation to the people of today.

The church, however, can do this only when she has a good and proper view of this prophetic and apostolic witness. But exactly here we encounter the great problem of our day. For many, many centuries there was complete unanimity on this point. Even the Reformation did not break up this unanimity. On the contrary! Although there were many sharp differences between Rome and the Reformation, even concerning the place and function of the

---

[4]P.T. Forsyth, *op. cit.,* 6. Cf. also the New Testament scholar Willi Marxsen who calls the New Testament "the oldest preserved sermon collection of the church" (Willi Marxsen, *Der Exeget als Theologe,* 1969, 126). Marxsen adds to these words: "but not the preaching text". According to him the preaching text lies behind the New Testment texts, although he does not deny that the latter, at least in part, has entered into the former. This, to me, is a false dilemma. Cf. also Werner Danielsmeyer, 'Der Text des Neuen Testaments als Grundlage unserer Predigt', *Monatschrift für Pastoraltheologie,* 50(1961), 193–201.

Bible in the church, they were nevertheless all agreed on the nature of Scripture. As far as this is concerned the *Second Helvetic Confession* spoke not only for the churches of the Reformation but for the Church of Rome as well, when it declared in its opening statement: "We believe and confess the canonical Scriptures of the holy prophets and apostles of both Testaments to be the true Word of God, and to have sufficient authority of themselves, not of men. For God himself spoke to the fathers, prophets, apostles, and still speaks to us through the Holy Scriptures."[4a]

In our day this situation has changed completely. Admittedly, Karl Barth and his followers have tried to recover and retain the idea of the Bible as the Word of God by actualizing it. Although in itself not more than a fallible human witness, the Bible may *become* the Word of God, "where and when it pleases God". But then it really *is* the Word of God. Within this context Barth did not hesitate to call the Bible the second form of the Word of God. Today, however, many theologians of the post-Barthian era are rather critical of this neo-orthodox view. James Barr, for instance, declares in the *Supplementary Volume* to *The Interpreter's Dictionary of the Bible*: "This scheme, for all its fine balance, has received less attention in recent years. Though theologically impressive, it has seemed to offer little help in solving actual interpretative problems within biblical scholarship."[5] In other words, the exegete cannot do much with this nice 'scheme'. Of course, Barr himself also sees the Bible as a special book. He is even prepared to speak of its authority, of the Bible as "something binding upon us".[6] Indeed, he even uses the term 'inspiration' again. "There must be some sense in which it is meaningful to say that it comes from God."[7] But all these terms are immediately thoroughly relativized, when he says that the concept of inspiration must be so framed as to accept the historical inaccuracies and contradictions in the Bible, yes even the theological imperfection,[8]

[4a]Arthur Cochrane, op. cit., 224.
[5]James Barr, in his article on 'Scripture, authority of', in *The Interpreter's Dictionary of the Bible (IDB), Supplementary Volume*, 1976, 795.
[6]*Art. cit.*, 795.
[7]*Art. cit.*, 794.
[8]*Art. cit.*, 794.

and when a little later he adds that authority does not exclude theological errors.[9]

Many other articles in the same dictionary, which in many ways is representative of present-day biblical scholarship, show a similar approach to Scripture. They speak of a rich pluralism within the Bible. By this term they mean that there are many, often conflicting theological standpoints in the Bible.[10] It is therefore necessary to apply 'content criticism' (German: *Sachkritik*) to the Bible. We may have to weigh Paul's words against what he says elsewhere, or we may have to evaluate various elements or stages of the gospel tradition against each other.[11] There is also much uncertainty as to the historical accounts of the Bible. "In some cases what actually happened may be quite different from any biblical account of it. For example, although we have four accounts of the trial of Jesus, what actually took place may have been quite different; after all, none of the disciples was there."[12]

☆   ☆   ☆

For those in the evangelical tradition such a view of Scripture and its authority is entirely unacceptable. The reason is not that they deny the problems posed by the exegesis of Scripture, but they believe that the only proper starting point for any doctrine of Scripture is that of *faith in Scripture*. Or to put it in other words, we have to begin with the *self-testimony* of Scripture itself.

There can be little doubt what this self-testimony is. Orthodoxy has always pointed quite rightly to the attitude

---

[9]*Art. cit.*, 795.
[10]L.E. Keck and G.M. Tucker, in their article on 'Exegesis', *IDB, Suppl. Vol.*, 1976, 302ff. I give two quotations from page 302. "Critical exegesis has shown that the Bible includes not only a long development but a rich pluralism, and that both Testaments contain internal critiques." "Critical exegesis has made it impossible to speak of *the* theology of the OT or the NT. Attempts to ascertain a single overarching theme, such as 'salvation history', or a particular understanding of human existence, do not justice to the whole range of biblical material; they only express particular viewpoints in modern theology."
[11]*Art. cit.*, 301.
[12]*Art. cit.*, 301.

of Christ to the Scriptures of the Old Testament. It is clear
from the Gospels that he unquestioningly accepted these
Scriptures as the authoritative Word of God. The same
attitude is taken by the apostles and the other authors of the
New Testament. There are even within the New Testament
itself some very clear, unambiguous statements about the
origin, nature and purpose of the Old Testament Scriptures,
which the church through the centuries has regarded as
decisive. We may cite 2 Tim. 3:16 – "All Scripture is inspired
of God", and 2 Peter 1:21 – "No prophecy ever came by the
impulse of man, but men moved by the Holy Spirit spoke
from God." The last passage in particular is important. It
says that these men, moved by the Spirit (literally: born
along by him, as a ship by the wind) spoke "from God" (*apo
theou*). Their message did not originate in their own heart,
but its origin was in God Himself. On the basis of all these
data only one conclusion is possible. We must maintain that
the Spirit so guided these writers, not only in their intentions but also in the results of their labour, that what they
wrote is the fully reliable and necessary foundation of the
church and the highest and decisive norm for its faith and
life.

Yet this is not all that is to be said here. However true it is
that the Bible is the *very Word of God* for us, at the same time
we must also acknowledge that it is the Word of God *in the
words of men*. The Bible was not written in heaven but on
earth. As Peter put it: *men* spoke from God. Some readers
may say: "But conservatives have never denied this". This is
true. But it is equally true that they often neglected or even
refused to draw the appropriate consequences from it. Too
often they virtually held a mechanical view of inspiration,
even though with their mouths they confessed an organic
view. Usually this became particularly manifest in their
interpretation of the historical parts of Scripture. Too often
'historical' was identified with literal accuracy.[13] In recent
years it has increasingly become evident that such a view is

[13]In 1926 there was a controversy about the interpretation of Gen. 3 in my own
denomination, the Reformed Churches in the Netherlands. Synod solved the
problem by declaring that the trees and the serpent in Gen. 3 were "observable by
sensory perception".

untenable. Take, for instance, the words and/or deeds of our Lord. There are obvious differences between the various accounts in the four Gospels. The Lord's Prayer is recorded in two different versions. The so-called Sermon on the Mount as recorded by Matthew differs in many details from what we read in Luke. While the Synoptic Gospels record the cleansing of the temple at the end of Jesus' ministry, the Gospel of John records it at the beginning. In the past, conservatives were inclined to explain these differences by assuming that Jesus would have spoken similar words on different occasions or that there would have been two cleansings of the temple. Today we should nearly all agree that this is a highly improbable solution. We have come to realize more and more that the Gospel writers were not notaries public, but, under the guidance of the Spirit, they had the freedom to record the words and deeds of Christ in such a way that the proclamation of the gospel was the better served. In fact, we begin to realize more and more that the composition of many books of the Bible, especially of the Old Testament, has been a very complicated affair. In many cases these books are the final result of a long historical tradition, which may have been oral, or written, or both.

✿   ✿   ✿

In recent years this realization has led many conservative scholars to a more positive appreciation of the so-called *historical-critical research of Scripture*.[14] In the past, the conservative attitude to this kind of research was generally very hostile. This was not surprising either, for the presuppositions of many critics were wholly unscriptural (usually they were both positivistic and evolutionary in nature) leading as a consequence to very negative results. The recent change in attitude among conservatives has several grounds.

(1) We have come to realize more and more that *all* sound

---

[14]Cf. George Eldon Ladd, *The New Testament and Criticism*, 1967. K. Runia, *Prediking en Historisch-Kritisch Onderzoek*, 1972. *New Testament interpretation. Essays on Principles and Methods* (ed. by I. Howard Marshall), 1977.

exegesis is critical in nature. Exegesis always means "comparison and judgment based on publicly accessible evidence and principles".[15] As a matter of fact, conservative scholars have always used these very same means and, like other exegetes, have often reached differing conclusions, for the simple reason that they "weighed the evidence differently and had varying sensibilities and insights".[16]

(2) We have discovered that most of the presuppositions and assumptions underlying the older and the current historical criticisms are not essential to and inherent in the historical-critical method as such, but are the result of the theological and philosophical ideas which the scholars themselves bring to and introduce within their research.[17]

(3) We have discovered that historical criticism, no less than literary criticism, has enriched our understanding of Scripture. Here we can mention only a few points.

(a) It appears that the vast majority of the Bible books have a *long and complicated history* behind them. Or to put it differently, many texts are actually multi-layered. This is quite evident in the Synoptic Gospels. Assuming that the Gospel according to Mark is the oldest Gospel we know, we must conclude that both Matthew and Luke have made use of Mark. But Mark himself made use of the preceding oral tradition, which in many ways was a preaching tradition. This oral tradition, in its turn, goes back to Jesus himself. In the Old Testament we find similar situations. The author of Chronicles undoubtedly made use of the existent books of Samuel and Kings. The authors of these books, in their turn, made use of earlier written and oral traditions. Sometimes we can clearly observe how the final authors and/or redactors have used their sources, and this can give us a much clearer insight into the intentions of the final author and/or

---

[15]Article on 'Exegesis' in *IDB, Suppl. Vol.*, 297.

[16]Art. cit., 297.

[17]In his article on 'Form Criticism, OT' G.M. Tucker righly writes: "It is a procedure, not a theology or an ideology, although it, like any other method, will entail a certain hermeneutic of language and particular assumptions concerning man, the world, knowledge, and perhaps even God" (*IDB, Suppl. Vol.*, 342). This is undoubtedly true, but it is equally true that the contents of these assumptions are largely determined by the *total* theology (or philosophy or ideology) of the exegete.

redactor. In other words, we get a much better understanding of the Bible text, on which we have to preach!

(b) It further appears that the author in his writing always had a *certain community of believers in view* and wanted to offer a *response to concrete occasions* in the life of this community. Even when he used existent material, either in written or in oral form, he rarely contented himself with simply copying this material, but he usually selected, ordered, reshaped and interpreted it in order to meet the needs of the community. The Gospels, for example, are not simply collections of existent traditions about Jesus, but each evangelist used the material in such a way that it met the needs of the community for which he wrote. The Pauline Epistles, without a single exception (not even the Epistle to the Romans!) are all occasional letters, i.e., letters occasioned by certain conditions, sometimes even crises, in the churches. The historical books of the Old Testament, too, show the same feature. They are not simply historical records of past events in the life of Israel, but each author used, ordered, reshaped the existent material in such a way that it contained a clear message for the believing community of his own day. At later stages the books often went through several redactions, which usually meant an actualizing or even re-actualizing of older materials for the sake of the believers of the new period.[18] It will be evident again that it will greatly enrich our preaching, when we can discover how and for what purpose the final redactor shaped the material in this particular way.

(c) Another important contribution made by historical criticism is the insight that the writers often used existing church traditions *against* the church. Leander E. Keck has emphasized this strongly in his book, *The Bible in the Pulpit.* He even calls the Bible an "anti-church book".[19] "Anti-church", as used by him, does not mean sheer hostility, but "a trenchant critique of the church as it was actually developing". In this sense one could call the New Testament "a series of twenty-seven minority reports". The New Testament writers do not simply record or repeat the tradition of

[18]We shall discuss this at greater length in Chapter V.
[19]Leander E. Keck, *op. cit.,* 1978, 90.

the young church, but use this tradition as a fundamental critique of what is happening in the young church. Again, it is evident how fruitful this insight will be for our present-day preaching of the Gospel. Today's minister should follow this example and confront his congregation in the same way with the biblical tradition as a critique.

We realize, of course, that making use of the various critical methods makes the exegetical task of the minister much more difficult and exacting. But we also believe that it becomes much more rewarding. In many cases the message, peculiar to this particular text, will come out much more clearly. In the past conservative/evangelical preaching has too often been superficial. The words of a particular text (quite often a very short text was chosen, sometimes only one verse or even a part of one verse) were used more or less at face value, and the real message was inspired by the minister's own doctrinal insights rather than by the actual message of the text itself. Whatever our critique of the newer exegetical methods may be, it cannot be denied that they compel us to study our text carefully and to wrestle with it until it has given us its own particular message. We are forced to dig into the text until we have found an answer to such questions as: Why did the author write as he did? What did he want to communicate to his readers in their particular situation? Today's preacher can become a truly biblical preacher only when he takes these questions utterly seriously.

☆   ☆   ☆

The clause, 'whatever our critique of the newer exegetical methods may be', demands some explanation: it would be regrettable if the argument so far had created the impression that I recommend the acceptance of the historical-critical methods lock, stock and barrel. As a matter of fact, I do not recommend this at all. As has already been stated, these methods are often used within a framework of theological and/or philosophical presuppositions and assumptions which are foreign to, or even worse, which are inimical to the very nature of the Scriptures. We have already referred to the denial of the unity of the Scriptures and to the relativizing of their inspiration and authority by many contemporary theologians. They simply accept a theological pluralism in Scripture and therefore see it as the task of the exegete to resort to what they call 'content criticism' (German: *Sachkritik*) of the Scriptures.

All this is usually connected with some other presuppositions and assumptions. In spite of the failure of both the old[20] and the new[21] quest for the historical Jesus, it is still quite common for critical scholars to defend the thesis that the *actual message lies behind the text*. In recent years this has been strongly advocated by *Wolfhart Pannenberg*.[22] He sees two big differences between Luther (and the Reformers in general) and us. Luther still believed in the clarity or perspicuity of Scripture, i.e. he believed that the most important or essential content (German: *die Sache*) arises clearly and univocally from its words, when they are expounded in accord with sound principles.[23] According to Pannenberg we can no longer uphold this. In the first place, we have discovered the distance between the intellectual milieu of the text and that of our own time. Secondly, we have also discovered that we have to distinguish between the attested events themselves and the tendencies in the reporting of the individual biblical writers. This second discovery means that the 'essential content', the '*Sache*' of Luther, *viz.* the person and history of Jesus, is no longer to be found *in* the texts themselves, but must be discovered *behind* them.[24]

We believe that this whole approach is impossible and fruitless. In the Bible *event and interpretation* are *inseparable*. We know the events only in and by means of the interpretative accounts, and these interpretative accounts are accounts

---

[20]Cf. A. Schweitzer, *The Quest of the Historical Jesus*, 2nd edition, 1931.

[21]Cf. the section on the historical Jesus question, in *IDB, Suppl. Vol.*, 103f., which begins with the words: "The failure to achieve clear results in the so called new quest of the historical Jesus".

[22]Cf. his article 'The Crisis of the Scripture Principle', in *Basic Questions in Theology*, Vol. I, 1970, 1–14.

[23]*Op. cit.*, 5.

[24]*Op. cit.*, 7.

of the events. So far as the so-called historical Jesus is concerned, we cannot possibly separate him from the Christ of faith who is proclaimed by the New Testament writers. Keck, who believes that the historical Jesus can be preached "as a catalytic question, as one who sets in motion reflection about the deepest questions of life before God and who calls for response"[25], nevertheless has to admit: "The Evangelists of course did not present the historical Jesus in distinction from the church's traditions about Jesus – for the simple reason that the distinction never occurred to them and that a historically ascertained (in our sense) Jesus was not available to them even if it had." But if this is true, how then should such a historical Jesus ever be available to us who are historically so much further removed from this Jesus? And even if our modern methods allowed us to discover him (which in fact they do not)[26] what would be the use of this Jesus if he is separated from the Christ of faith? Moreover, would not the historical Jesus likewise demand faith in himself as the One sent by God? Would this not mean that even *as* the historical Jesus he always *is* the Christ of faith?

Connected with the foregoing is the view, quite common among the critics, that the preacher can and may preach on any of the *layers of* tradition which he finds behind the present text. Kurt Frör, for example, says concerning the multi-layered tradition of the Old Testament that there are several possibilities for the preacher. He can take the oldest layer, i.e., the text as it lies before us. Or he can choose to show the congregation that there are several layers, i.e., he can preach on the developing text.[27] The same would apply to the New Testament.[28] The preacher can take the final text of Matthew or Luke, or he can go back to Mark, or to Q (= *Quelle* – source), or – behind this – to the oral tradition, or to

---

[25]Leander E. Keck, *op. cit.*, 135. He goes on to say that "the historical Jesus can elicit this questioning precisely where the church's Christ wouldn't even get a hearing" and mentions as an impressive illustration "the beautiful book" by the Marxist Milan Machovec: *A Marxist Looks at Jesus*, 1976.

[26]Cf. the article on 'Biblical Criticism NT', in *IDB Suppl. Vol.*, 103f.

[27]Kurt Frör, *Biblische Hermenutik. Zur Schriftauslegung in Predigt und Unterricht*, 1964, 151. It should be noted that Frör also calls for caution. "We should not make such attempts rashly, Luke 14:28." As a matter of fact, the general rule should be to use the final form, i.e., the present text.

[28]*Op. cit.*, 250f.

the early Christian prophecy, or to the words of the historical Jesus.[29] But how must the preacher choose? The criterion
cannot simply be the historical aspect. Frör himself rejects
the contrasts authentic-unauthentic, earlier-later, original-
secondary as invalid. Not even the *ipsissima vox Jesu* (the
actual words of Jesus) is decisive. Frör himself recommends
a twofold criterion. 1. Content criticism. The preacher must
ask himself which layer of the tradition does most justice to
the *Sache* (the essential content) with which the New
Testament is concerned. 2. The situation of the congregation. The preacher must ask himself which layer of the
tradition shows a situation that is most analogous to the
situation of his own congregation.[30]
    We believe that there are several *serious objections* against
this view. (1) Who is going to decide what is the *Sache*? Is it
Frör? Is it you? Is it me? But on what basis are we to decide?
Frör himself rejects the idea of a 'canon within the canon'
(e.g., Luther's doctrine of justification). But can he really
avoid this solution? Does he not have to determine, one way
or another, what is the *Sache* in order to apply this to the
various layers? But does this not lead to the famous vicious
circle? (2) We may not forget that Tradition Criticism often is
little more than a matter of scholarly hypothesis. Only rarely
do we have absolute certainty. It is therefore not surprising
to see that quite often different scholars arrive at different
results. But can one preach God's Word on the basis of a
scholarly hypothesis? (3) If we select earlier layers we will
preach on something that is *not* in the text. At times it may
even mean that we will have to preach on something that is
quite different from what the present text says. Supposing,
for instance, one wants to preach on the earlier layers of
Gen. 32:22–32, as these are assumed by many scholars?
According to them the original story is a pre-Israelite saga
about some river-demon. The next stage would be a story
about Jacob meeting a strange, daemonic power, called El,
which threatens to kill him, but which is conquered by

---

[29]*Op. cit.,* 251 Cf. also Leander E. Keck, *op. cit.,* 110, 134.
[30]*Op. cit.,* 252. Cf. also L. E. Keck and G. M. Tucker, article on 'Exegesis' in *IDB,*
Suppl. Vol., 303, and Friedrich Winter in the section on 'Die Predigt', in *Handbuch*
der Praktischen Theologie (produced by Heinrich Ammer a.o.), Vol. II, 1974, 248ff.

Jacob. The following stage would be the story of a mysterious encounter between Jacob and Yahweh who blesses
Jacob before he re-enters the promised land.[31] But can a
preacher really preach on the first two layers, when it is clear
that the final layer (i.e. the text as it now stands) completely
discards all references to a river-demon or a strange, daemonic power? Would preaching on the earlier layers not be
disobedience to the sacred text as it has been delivered to us
under the guidance of the Holy Spirit? In my opinion there
is *only one preaching text,* namely, the canonical Bible text. It
was apparently the intention of the Holy Spirit to give this
text to the church on its journey through the ages. In this text
we find the message which the church of all ages needs. This
does not mean that all traditio-critical research is useless.
Even though its results are largely hypothetical, especially
where very early traditions are concerned, they do have a
certain value, in particular when they enable us to see more
clearly how and why the final text received its present form.
Such an insight often gives the preacher a clue how today he
must actualize or even re-actualize the message of the text.

✻   ✻   ✻

In this connection, we cannot pass by the latest developments in the field of exegesis. Under the influence of
modern linguistics and following the impact of present-day
liberation movements, a new exegetical method is becoming
very popular, namely, *structuralism.* In many ways this new
method is also a reaction to the often hypothetical and
purely academic results of historical criticism. The structuralists concentrate on the text as it lies before us.[32] Contrary to

[31]Cf. J. de Fraine S. J., *Genesis uit de grondtekst vertaald en uitgelegd,* 1963, *ad locum.*
Cf. also P.A.H. de Boer, 'Genesis XXXII 23–33, some remarks on composition and
character of the story', *Nederlands Theologisch Tijdschrift,* I(1946), 149–163; F. van
Trigt, 'La signification de la lutte de Jacob près du Yabboq, Gen. XXXII 23–33', *Old
Testament Studies,* XII (1958), 280–309.
[32]For a list of general works on structuralism, see the bibliography in *IDB, Suppl.
Vol.,* 551 (article on 'Literature, the Bible as', by D. Robertson). For a more
theological approach, see the collection of essays in *Interpretation* Vol. 28 (1974),
April issue; D.O. Via, Jr., *Kerygma and Comedy in the New Testament: A Structuralist*

the form-critical and traditio-critical scholars who dissect the text into smaller units and trace the separate meanings of these units, the structuralists want to study the text as a whole by showing the interrelation of the units. In many ways this seems to be a wholesome reaction to the fragmentation of the text which is so characteristic of the historical-critical method. It most certainly appeals to conservative scholarship which has always been primarily interested in the message of the canonical text. On the other hand, conservative scholars should realize that most structuralists also have a low view of Scripture and share many of the assumptions of their critical counterparts. Moreover, many structuralists appear to use this method to defend the basic tenets of modern liberation theology. In many instances structuralism allies itself with the so-called materialistic exegesis,[33] which usually leads to new distortions of the biblical message.

☆   ☆   ☆

So far we have dealt mainly with views that are not acceptable to evangelicals and it is easy to shoot arrows at distant targets! But what about conservative and evangelical Christians? Do they really understand the *biblical message*? When I read collections of sermons published within the evangelical community, I have serious doubts. Of course, there are many sound evangelical and biblical insights and statements in these sermons. Yet on the whole they are disappointing. Sometimes they even deal with their text in an altogether unbiblical way, namely, by using nearly all texts in an anthropocentric, exemplaristic, and consequently moralizing way. Apparently a high view of Scripture does not automatically result in the right use of Scripture!

Approach to Hermeneutic, 1975; C.J. den Heyer, *Exegetische methoden in discussie*, 1978.
[33]See, e.g., Fernando Belo, *Lecture Matérialiste de l'évangile de Marc*, 1974; Michel Clévenot, *Approches matérialistes de la Bible*, 1976; the special issue of *Movement* (magazine of the British S.C.M.), September 1977, with contributions by Pablo Richard and Gabriele Dietrich.

Personally I believe that the only proper way of reading (and therefore preaching) the Bible is to read it in terms of *salvation history* or *redemptive history (Heilsgeschichte)*. The Bible is the witness of prophets and apostles to the self-revelation of the God of Israel and the Father of Jesus Christ. In it we read how the God in whom Israel believed and whom Jesus Christ called his Father, revealed himself as the Saviour and Judge in the history of the covenant people of old and in particular in the life, death and resurrection of Jesus Christ.

It is true that in recent biblical theology this salvation-history approach has again fallen on evil times.[34] After the strong emphasis on the idea of 'revelation in history' in the biblical theology of the period after World World II (in the writings of e.g. Cullmann, Wright, Von Rad, Ridderbos,) recent biblical theology has begun to question this whole expression. It believes that too many ambiguities surround it. James Barr mentions several, such as: ambiguities about the nature of the revelatory events, about the sense of 'history', about the relation between revelation and history, and about the relation between revelation and the biblical text itself. This is quite an impressive list, and conservatives too have to take these problems seriously. I believe Barr is right in pointing out that the concept of revelation is much more complex than was often assumed in the past. Yet I would maintain also that this complexity may never be used to deny that God has revealed himself in the history of Israel and of Jesus Christ. And whatever ambiguities there may be, they do not alter the fact that God's self-revelation was always of two kinds: it was revelation by both word and deed. It may well be that the one-sided concentration of the earlier biblical theology on the revelation in the events of history has led to the recent demise of the concept of 'revelation in history'. Too often the assumption was that the real revelation was in the historical event and that the interpretation was added afterwards. This, however, is contrary to the biblical records themselves. They do not recognize *'nuda facta'*, bare facts, which afterwards were

---

[34]Cf. the article on 'Revelation in history', by James Barr, in *IDB, Suppl. Vol.*, 746–749.

interpreted so that they became facts of salvation. On the contrary, the interpretation is always seen as the un-folding of the facts themselves. The revelatory quality is the secret that is present in the event itself, and it only becomes manifest in the interpretation.

Take, for instance, the Exodus. It is not true that a band of Israelites managed to escape from Egypt and that these people *afterwards*, when they began to reflect on this event, interpreted it as a revelation of God's saving power, but from the very start this Exodus is seen as God's saving deed. In the case of the Exodus we even see that God *beforehand* announced to his servant Moses that he was going to redeem Israel (Ex. 3:7ff.). As a matter of fact, this is not an exception, but it is the normal pattern in the Old Testament. The prophetic word always precedes God's acting in history.[35] And even when the Old Testament does not deal explicitly with God's own acts in the history of Israel, but rather gives a prophetic, *a posteriori* interpretation of Israel's history (as we find this, for instance, in the great historical books, such as Joshua-Kings and Chronicles-Ezra), this interpretation is not read *into* the facts, but it is derived from the facts, as they are seen in the broad framework of God's covenant with Israel.

[35]Claus Westermann says: "One can speak meaningfully about this intervention of God in history if it is connected with the Word. Those who experienced the deliverane at the Red Sea, and later generations, could *not* confess, praise, and pass on this event as an act of God, solely because they *believed* God had acted, or because they had a conviction or a feeling. They could do this only for the *sole* reason that this salvation had word-character, i.e., because this deliverance was promised them in the hour of distress, and they could therefore experience it as fulfilment of the promise, or as the happening of the predicted. This connection is of decisive importance for the understanding of the Old Testament. The fact that a historical event is witnessed to be an act of God can in the Old Testament never – at least never exclusively – be proved because the people who were involved had certain thoughts, experiences, or beliefs. This is not a sufficient foundation to carry a creed! Rather the only basis for a creed is this: that a *factum* is recognized as a *dictum*. The saving act at the Red Sea *began* with this – that a Word came to a man (Exod. 3: 7f.): 'I have *seen* the affliction of my people who are in Egypt, and have *heard* their cry because of their taskmaster; I know their sufferings, and I *have come down to deliver them out of the hand of the Egyptians....'" Claus Westermann, 'The Interpretation of the Old Testament', in *Essays on Old Testament Interpretation (ed. by Claus Westermann), 1963, 47f.* Cf. also W. Pannenberg in *Revelation as History* (ed. by W. Pannenberg), 1968, 153: "The prophetic word precedes the act of history, and these acts are understandable as acts of Yahweh only because a statement coming in the name of Yahweh interprets them this way."

The same is true of the New Testament. There we find the same inseparable connection between event and interpretation. Whether it is *a priori* interpretation or *a posteriori* interpretation (and the latter undoubtedly predominates in the New Testament), in both cases the interpretation does not add something to the event that was not present in the event itself, but it is based on either the content or the context of the event. H.M. Kuitert rightly points out that the New Testament writers did not arbitrarily *attribute* a wonderful significance to Jesus but rather *derived* this significance from the person and work of Jesus himself. "The affair (= *die Sache*) itself and its significance are interwoven: the event does not stand apart from its significance. The interpretation of Jesus, his way and his work as the way of salvation ... comes from Jesus Himself ... Paul did not damage what Jesus accomplished. In his own way – and his way is different from that of John or the writer of Hebrews, and is more explicit than that of Jesus Himself – Paul illuminated Jesus in his person and work by means of the person and work itself."[36] Kuitert refers here in particular to the New Testament Epistles, but the same is true of the interpretative elements in the Gospels.[37]

✿   ✿   ✿

This basic structure of the Bible naturally has important *consequences* for the way we read the Bible and, therefore, also for our preaching.

1. In the first place, it means that the biblical message is *theocentric* in nature. Even though the deeds and words of men and women fill the greater part of the Bible, the real centre is what God does and says. Therefore, a sermon that entirely concentrates on the people mentioned in the text, on

---

[36]H.M. Kuitert, *The Reality of Faith*, 1968, 167.

[37]Cf. also Alan Richardson, *Introduction to the Theology of the New Testament*, 1958. In another book he himself describes this Introduction as an attempt to show "that the theology of the New Testament as a whole is based primarily upon Jesus' own interpretation of his mission and person in the light of his understanding of the Old Testament", *History, sacred and profane*, 1964, 141/2.

what they do and say, is, in spite of all its good intentions, basically unbiblical. As a matter of fact, such a sermon usually amounts to little else than a moralizing address.

2. The biblical message has a basically *redemptive-historical* structure. To be sure, there are parts of the Bible that seem to lack this structure (e.g., the Psalms and the Wisdom literature), but even they have to be read against the background and within the framework of the all-overarching redemptive-historical structure. The only way to preach biblically is to recognize that "the unifying structure of Scripture is that of redemptive history ... Biblical theology both recognizes the unity and epochal structure of this history." Careful study of each period "in its own context and 'theological horizon'", shows that "each epoch has a coherent and organic structure and also that there is organic progression from period to period as the plan of God is revealed".[38] In other words, each passage has to be seen in its proper place in this history of salvation.

3. It follows from the foregoing that our reading of and preaching on the Bible must be *christocentric*. This third aspect represents not an addition to the theocentric nature and redemptive-historical structure of the biblical revelation, but rather constitutes their accentuation and focalization. The God about whom we hear in the Bible is the Father of Jesus Christ and the redemptive history of which the Bible speaks has its very centre in the life, death and resurrection of Jesus Christ. Karl Barth was absolutely right when he said that the whole Bible is a witness to Christ, the Old Testament pointing forward to him and the New Testament pointing back to him. Or to put it in the words of Von Rad: our point of departure must always be "the belief that the same God who has revealed Himself in Christ has also left his footsteps in the history of the Old Testament covenant people – that we have to do with *one* divine discourse, here to the fathers through the prophets, there to us through Christ (Heb. 1:1)".[39] No sermon therefore is truly biblical which does not show that the text as part of the

[38]Edmund P. Clowney, *Preaching and Biblical Theology*, 1962, 75; cf. 16ff.

[39]Gerhard von Rad, 'Typological Interpretation of the Old Testament', in *Essays on Old Testament Interpretation* (ed. by Claus Westermann), 1963, 36.

redemptive-historical revelation of God points to Christ as being the very heart of this revelation.

The question may arise here, whether in this way we can still do justice to the *human aspect* of this history of salvation. Is it not true that men and women are also involved and that they even play a very important part in the biblical texts? This is undoubtedly true and we may not and cannot ignore it. It is an indispensable aspect of revelation as redemptive-historical revelation. The God in whom we believe is the Covenant God, who wants to be the Covenant-partner of his people. When at the burning bush he gives the most profound self-revelation in the sacred Name *Yahweh* (Ex. 3:8), which means "I am who I am" or "I shall be who I shall be", this Name should not be interpreted in the abstract sense of "I am the Eternal One" (although this is also implied), but the correct interpretation is: "I am with you and shall ever be with you". And when this same God reveals himself in Jesus Christ, his incarnate Son, this revelation can be interpreted only as "*Immanuel*" – God with us (Matt. 1:23; cf. Is. 7:14). Karl Barth, therefore, was correct when he said that Christian theology is always 'theo-anthropology'.[40] Christian theology and Christian preaching are always about God and man at the same time. But – God comes first! It is always theo-anthropology and never the other way round! Salvation always comes *from* God and it comes *to* man. God himself is always the *Subject* of revelation and man is no more than the *addressee*. Yet even in this humble and subordinate role man is always present in the act of revelation and plays his own, indispensable part. This is also true of Christian preaching. Man is never the subject matter of preaching. We preach God's salvation in Jesus Christ. Yet man is never absent in this preaching, for God's salvation in Jesus Christ always concerns man and it always comes to him in his *concrete, historical situation*. Seen from this perspective man is the second focus in the ellipse of Christian preaching. In our next chapter we deal with this second focus.

[40]Karl Barth, *Evangelical Theology: An Introduction*, 1963, 12.

FOUR

Preaching and the Situation of the Listener

The last chapter started with the thesis that, if our preaching is to be *Christian* preaching, it has to be *biblical* preaching: we now add a second thesis. If our preaching is to be truly biblical preaching, it has to take the *listener* and *his situation* seriously. This thesis as such is not new either. The Christian church has always realised that it is not enough to expound a particular passage of Scripture. The message of this passage must also be *applied* to the present-day listener. In nearly all homiletical textbooks we read that preaching always means two things: first, the exposition and second, the application of a passage of Scripture. The books also show that the second task is at least as difficult as the first. In fact, most preachers find it the more demanding part of their sermon preparation.

The question we now face is:Does recent biblical research help us to gain a better understanding of this second focus of the ellipse of preaching?

✿   ✿   ✿

For a starting point we return to the view of *Karl Barth* and the reaction to this view by the younger, post-Barthian theologians in Germany. As we have already seen, Barth had a very high view of preaching. To him preaching was no less than the third form of the Word of God. Accordingly he put all emphasis on the *content* of the message. To him this was so decisive that he could declare: "Good dogmatics – good theology – good preaching."[1] Apparently he was aware of the questions such a statement might evoke, for he immediately added: "The suspicion and the reproach of 'hybris' (= pride) may seem unavoidable". Yet he did maintain it, for he was deeply convinced that the content really determines whether our dogmatics, our theology, and, therefore, our preaching also, are good or bad. And since it is especially the task of dogmatics to reflect on the content of the biblical message, dogmatics was for Barth the real heart of all theology and the determinative factor in all preaching. Furthermore, he was so deeply convinced that God alone can speak his own Word, that he had little or no interest in all our human attempts at communication. At times one even gets the impression that he saw all such attempts as obstacles to the effectiveness of God's Word. What are we to make, for instance, of the following statement: Practical Theology must not become involved in "the idle question of how those who proclaim this Word should 'approach' this or that modern man, or how they should 'bring home' the Word of God to him. Instead the real question is how they have to *serve* this Word by pointing to its coming. This Word has never been 'brought home' to any man except *by its own freedom and power*".[2] Of course, one cannot but agree with the latter part of this statement. Indeed, God always remains the Lord of his own Word. Only his Spirit can bring the message into the heart of the listener. But does this really mean that, therefore, the preacher does not have to do his utmost to bring the message as close to the heart of the listener as he possibly can? Is that really an 'idle' question?

The same problems arise when we examine what Barth says about the place and role of the situation of the listener in preaching. At first glance this may seem strange, because both in his *Church Dogmatics* and in his *Homiletics* he emphatically mentions this aspect. Take, for instance, the following statement from *Church Dogmatics* I 1: "The actual

[1] Karl Barth, *CD*, I, 2, 767.
[2] Karl Barth, *Evangelical Theology: An Introduction*, 1963, 182.

thing to be proclaimed we may not and cannot expect to hear from dogmatics. That must be found again and again in the middle between the particular text of the Bible within the context of the whole Bible and the congregation in its particular situation of the varying present."[3] Or take the short statement from his *Homiletics*: "Be faithful to the text and be faithful to life."[4] Such statements seem to leave no room for any doubt that Barth too wants to take the situation of the listener seriously. And yet the doubt lingers on. For there are too many other statements that rob the words just quoted of their real power and significance. When we take his theory of preaching in its entirety, we cannot avoid the conclusion that the historical situation of the listener does not play any constituent part in the preparation and delivery of the sermon. All the weight remains on the content of the message, and the situation can at most function as a sounding board for the message.

But there is still more to be said here. Barth's lack of real interest in the concrete, historical situation of the listener has a deeper reason. According to him this historical situation is not the *real* situation of man. The real situation is man's situation *before God*, a situation man does not know by himself, but can discover only when it is revealed to him in the proclamation itself! In his *Homiletics* Barth puts it thus: "A preacher is called to lead to God the people whom he sees before him; God desires him to preach to these people here present. But he must approach them as people who are already the object of God's action, for whom Christ died and has risen again. He has to tell them, therefore, that God's mercy avails for them as truly today as at the beginning of time. That is what is meant by adapting preaching to the congregation."[5] Here we are at the real heart of Barth's view of the situation. Compared with this *real* situation the concrete, historical situation is only relative and secondary. And this *real* situation, which is the same for all people of all times, must be announced in the sermon. To all and sundry it must be said: "You are a sinner, but God loves you in

---

[3]*CD*, I, 1, 89; cf. 64ff.
[4]Karl Barth, *Prayer and Preaching*, 1964, 109; cf. 106ff.
[5]Op. cit., 96.

Jesus Christ. Yes, in Jesus Christ he has already reconciled you to himself. Believe this Gospel and turn to Jesus Christ for your salvation." And so Barth can also say: "From beginning to end the Bible is concerned with one unique theme which is, however, presented in many different ways. As a result of this variety each passage, at every period, speaks to man's needs."[6] On another page he says that the movement of the sermon does "not consist so much in *going towards* men as in *coming from* Christ to meet them",[7] to which the German edition adds: "Then one goes *automatically* to man."[8]

☆   ☆   ☆

By its strong emphasis on the content of the message and on the divine promise that God will use our inadequate and powerless words as vehicles of his Word Barth's theory of preaching was a great *encouragement* to many preachers in the period between the two world wars and also for a considerable time after World War II. Walter Fürst, one of his former students, spoke on behalf of many colleagues when in 1963 he declared that Barth had given him and his fellow-students courage and joy to preach.[9]

At the same time, however, we are not surprised either that gradually a *reaction* set in. For Barth's theory may have been a correct and even a beautiful dogmatic theory, but the reality of preaching as it was going on Sunday after Sunday did not tally with it. In the appendix on 'Word of God and language', added to his book *The Nature of the Christian Faith*, Gerhard Ebeling wrote about the experience of many churchgoers that "the event of proclamation is not an event any more today, but largely just talk, in which the claim of the Word of God is no longer heard; it is proclamation in a

[6]*Op. cit.*, 90.
[7]*Op. cit.*, 71.
[8]Karl Barth, *Homiletik: Wesen und Vorbereitung der Predigt*, 1966, 38 (my emphasis, K.R.)
[9]Walter Fürst, 'Die homiletische Bedeutsamkeit Karl Barths', *Theologische Existenz Heute*, No. 104, 1963, 5.

form of language which has become incomprehensible, it is a mere recitation of the traditional Word of God, in which the Word of God does not enter language in the present."[10] Many similar criticisms were voiced by others. Increasingly the theologians, especially the practical theologians, became convinced that Barth's theory, however correct dogmatically, really ignores the specifically homiletic aspect of preaching. A minister is not called to preach the Word of God in general and in abstract, but it is his task to preach it to *a particular congregation in its own particular historical situation.*

In particular, *Ernst Lange,* a young German theologian, took up this homiletical challenge and developed a new theory of preaching in which the situation of the listener plays a constituent and even determinative part. Lange did not reject the Barthian thesis that God is always the Subject of his own Word and that it is never in man's power to speak this Word. In fact, he fully agreed with it. But what he did deny was that the historical situation of the listener is really irrelevant to the message. Lange vigorously maintained that without a clear relation to this historical situation the *message itself remains irrelevant!* The homiletical task of the minister is to show to the people that the Christian tradition, as embodied in the Bible, is relevant for their actual situation. Even though the minister begins with the text (as a Lutheran Lange followed the so-called pericope system), his actual starting point is the situation of the listener. Lange puts it very sharply thus: "He, the listener, is my theme."[11] I speak with him about his life, his experiences, etc. I hold his life, so to speak, in the light of the biblical message in order to show him the real truth of his life. It is obvious that the old distinction of exposition-application is useless for Lange. Preaching based on this distinction proceeds from the text, tries to formulate the message (or the *scopus* or the *kerygma* or whatever other term one wants to use) and only then turns to the situation. In other words, we already know what we have to say before we have even looked at the situation. Our preaching is virtually a one-way communication: from the text to the situation. But according to Lange

[10]Gerhard Ebeling, *op. cit.,* 1961, 184.
[11]Ernst Lange, *Predigen als Beruf,* 1976, 58.

this is not correct. We may not act as if the relevance for today is simply present in the text. We should realize that the situation of the text is a *past* situation. The original listeners are *not* the listeners of today's preacher. The preacher of today has to create the relevance by actualizing the Christian tradition for the present situation. This means that he has to examine the text carefully and select those elements which are potentially relevant for today. In some cases it may even mean that he has to go against the text or certain aspects of the text.[12]

We cannot go further into Lange's interesting theory. But it will already be obvious that he has introduced a very important issue, which had been unduly neglected in the Barthian theology. On the other hand, we may ask whether Lange's own theory does not perhaps go to the other extreme and virtually make the situation *the* determinative factor in the preaching event. In many ways his view reminds one of the so-called correlation method, which Paul Tillich introduced into systematic theology. He described it as follows: In using this method systematic theology "makes an analysis of the human situation out of which the existential questions arise, and it demonstrates that the symbols used in the Christian message are the answers to these questions".[13] The great problem of this method (and the same holds true of Lange's theory) is that to a large extent the answers are determined by the questions. It is not God's Word that puts the questions to man, so that man may discover his true situation, but the analysis of man's situation brings out the questions of man's existence, which then are answered by God's Word. To be honest, both Tillich and Lange do not deny that God's Word also supplements and corrects man's questions, but this does not really solve the problem. The basic starting point lies in the situation of man and the big question remains whether this method does not

[12]*Op. cit.*, 66.
[13]Paul Tillich, *Systematic Theology*, vol. I, 1951, 62; cf. the whole section, pp. 59–66. Cf. also his article 'Die Verkündigung des Evangeliums', in Paul Tillich, *Sammelte Werke*, Vol. III, 265–275.

unavoidably lead to a reduction of the message of Scripture.[14]

☆   ☆   ☆

Nevertheless, Lange has re-introduced a very important issue which every homiletical theory has to take into account. A Reformed theory of preaching, too, has to face this issue and must try to determine which part the situation of the listener has to play in the preaching event.

In point of fact, the *Bible* itself sheds much light on this issue. We have already noted an important characteristic of all the writings of the New Testament: that they were addressed to particular communities of believers and that they always tried to give a response to concrete issues in the life of these communities. The New Testament writings were not religious tracts in which the doctrine of God's salvation in Jesus Christ was expounded in a purely objective way, but occasional writings, prompted by a particular situation in the community and seeking to evaluate this situation in the light of God's saving action in Jesus Christ.

This is quite obvious in the case of Paul's letters. Every letter is an occasional writing prompted by the situation of the congregation concerned. In each case the apostle deals explicitly with this situation and expounds the gospel of Jesus Christ in such a way that the situation is really illuminated by the gospel, either positively or negatively. Thus in the letter to the Galatians the gospel is expounded within the framework of the controversy about circumcision, and the apostle uses the opportunity to deal with the whole problem of the Mosaic law in relation to Jesus Christ. In the letters to the Thessalonians the situation prompts Paul

---

[14]Cf. e.g., Alexander J. McKelway, *The Systematic Theology of Paul Tillich,* 1964, passim. In his Introductory Report to this volume Karl Barth asks some pertinent questions: "Is man with his philosophical questions, for Tillich, not more than simply the beginning point of the development of this whole method of correlation? Is he not, in that he himself knows which questions to ask, anticipating their correctness, and therefore already in possession of the answers and their consequences?", *op. cit.,* 13.

to deal extensively with the Second Coming of the Lord. The letters to the Ephesians and the Colossians deal with the relation of Christ to the church and with the so-called 'Haustafel', the codes of household duties, in which the apostle gives guidelines to special groups in the congregation. Of particular interest are the two letters to the congregation at Corinth. Paul had a very close relationship with this congregation, as it had been established by his own preaching during a stay of about eighteen months in this city. Both letters, but in particular the first, deal with a host of problems that are present in the congregation.[15] At the same time they also give us a clear idea of *how Paul would have preached* in the congregation. He would not have given a general address of a rather objectivizing nature on the Christ-event, but taking his point of departure in this event he would have tackled the concrete problems of the congregation in the light of this event. This is not just my own hypothesis, but it is clearly proved by the letters themselves. It is scarcely going too far to say that they are nothing else than the written form of what Paul would have said to the congregation had he been on the scene.[16] Indeed, even in their written form they functioned in a way as sermonic material, because they were read aloud during the worship service of the congregation (cf. Col. 4:16).

The same is true of the non-Pauline Epistles in the New Testament. Every introduction to the New Testament tells us that in the case of each letter we can deduce from its content which problems were present in the congregation concerned. We usually speak of "general" epistles, but in actual fact they are not so general at all. Most of them clearly deal with particular problems of the communities addressed. It is further generally believed that the Epistle to the Hebrews is an expanded sermon. But the Gospels too, although they have a more objective nature, clearly show that they were written for certain communities of believers in their particu-

---

[15]Such as: divisions within the congregation; a case of incest; going to law with each other; sexual impurity; questions about marriage and celibacy; questions about food offered to idols; abuses in connection with the Lord's Supper; denial of the final resurrection; confusion concerning the spiritual gifts; etc.

[16]Leander E. Keck, *op. cit.*, 84.

lar situation. K. Weiss may overaccentuate this point when he says concerning the Gospel of Mark that "the centre of gravity does not lie in the christological instruction but in the ecclesiological admonition", but he is certainly right when he observes that "from the literary point of view the borderline between the genres of Gospel and Epistle becomes somewhat vague".[17]

Finally, with regard to the Old Testament we discover the same process. It may be more complex, but it is not basically different. "The complexity is greater partly because the books were produced across a much longer time span, and partly because some of the Wisdom materials and the Song of Songs may have been generated primarily out of the creative impulses of gifted individuals instead of being produced for community use at the outset. Still, when all this is taken into account, the tapestry is richer and more varied, but the broad design is the same: the books of this part of the Bible too were generated by particular occasions in the life of the community."[18]

✳   ✳   ✳

What does all this mean for *our present-day preaching?* I think that our preaching should happen along the same lines. We too should realize that the living Word of God always occurs *at the point of intersection* of the message of the text with the concrete situation of those who hear the message. Today too, the message of Scripture becomes fruitful for preaching only when the minister, in solidarity with his congregation, tries to accomplish this intersecting. How he has to do this he does not know beforehand. He can find this out only by reflecting carefully on both his text and his congregation. What the result of this reflection will be he does not know beforehand either. In some cases he will

---

[17]K. Weiss, in *Der historische Jesus under der kerygmatische Christus. Beiträge sum Christusverständnis in Forschung und Verkündigung* (ed. by H. Ristow and K. Matthiae), 1962, 425f.

[18]Leander E. Keck, *op. cit.*, 85; cf. 114f.

discover that the text contains a truly comforting message for the congregation, namely, when the situation of the congregation really calls for comfort. But quite often he will discover that the message of the text challenges prevailing understandings and loyalties in the congregation, because these understandings and loyalties do not have their origin in the Gospel but in purely worldly conceptions and attitudes. Obviously, such a challenging preaching may easily lead to irritation or even hostility on the side of the congregation. But the faithful preacher must not try to avoid this – even though he should constantly be alert to the possibility that it is not the Gospel that challenges the congregation but his own pet theological, social or political ideas!

It would be hard to over-emphasize how decisive the situation is in actualizing the message of the text. A different situation will lead to an entirely different actualization. Willi Marxsen once made this clear by the simple example of two hypothetical letters written by a father to his son. The first starts as follows: "I am rather amazed to hear that you want to get married. I think you haven't thought enough about it … etc," The second begins with the words: "I was very happy to receive the invitation to your wedding … etc." Are these two letters contradictory? That need not be so when, for instance, the one son is eighteen years old and the other twenty-six, or when a period of about eight years separates the two letters to the same son. Marxsen rightly concludes from this that the correctness of a statement does not simply lie in the statement itself. The correctness is co-determined by the situation for which the statement is made.[19]

This point can easily be proved by examples from Scripture itself. Consider, for instance, Isaiah 51:2, 3 compared with Ezek. 33:24. In both texts the same argument is used, but it is used quite differently and the difference is determined by the situation! In Ezekiel 33 the exiles in Babylon hear of the fall of Jerusalem. Instead of seeing it as God's judgment they console themselves by quoting an old tradition about Abraham: "Abraham was only one man; yet he got possession of the land; but we are many; the land is surely given us to possess." In the name of the Lord Ezekiel

---

[19]Willi Marxsen, *op. cit.*, 63.

rejects this appeal to the old promise. Without repentance on the side of the people the promise will not only not come true but every appeal to it is a lie. But when we turn to Isaiah 51, we find quite a different picture. The descendants of the same exiles of Ezekiel's days have become despondent and have lost all courage and faith. And then we notice the remarkable fact that Isaiah appeals to the very same tradition and uses it as a new promise of comfort: "Look to Abraham your father and to Sarah who bore you; for when he was but one I called him, and I blessed him and made him many. For the Lord will comfort Zion; he will comfort all her waste places, and will make her wilderness like Eden, her desert like the garden of the Lord; joy and gladness will be found in her, thanksgiving and the voice of song."[20]

It is clear from this example that the use of a message is co-determined by the situation of the congregation. Indeed, the difference is so important that it can determine whether a preacher is a true or a false prophet! An example of this is found in Jeremiah 28, where we read of the dispute between Hananiah of Gibeon and Jeremiah. Both belonged to the prophetic order. In the first verses of the chapter Hananiah promises the people that within two years all the vessels of the temple and also the exiles themselves will be returned to Jerusalem. Undoubtedly Hananiah based this prophecy on the promises about the land and the temple which God had given in the past. Jeremiah, however, opposes him. Certainly he also would like Hananiah's words to be fulfilled. But seeing the unrepentant attitude of the people he knows that the promises of God (which he does not dispute) cannot apply in this situation. J.N. Sanders, who mentions this example, rightly quotes the words of Eva Oswald: "The true prophet must be able to distinguish whether a historical hour stands under the wrath or the love of God."[21] The same applies to the true preacher of today.

✽ ✽ ✽

[20]Cf. J.A. Sanders, article on 'Hermeneutics', in *IDB, Suppl. Vol.*, 404.
[21]*Art. cit.*, 405.

All this leads me to still another point. Taking careful account of the situation of the congregation may also be an important means *to avoid moralizing in our preaching*. Moralizing usually has two sources. The one is an anthropocentric approach to the biblical texts; instead of approaching the text from the perspective of its place in the history of redemption, the preacher concentrates entirely on the words and actions of the people in the text, the result being that these people themselves become models for morality, either positively or negatively. The congregation is called to act like them, or when their actions are sinful, not to act like them. Joseph, for instance, becomes the great example of faith, of honesty, of moral purity, etc. But the preacher ignores completely the fact that the author of the book of Genesis puts the story of Joseph within the framework of the history of salvation and that every part of this story must be preached within this very framework. The key to the whole story is found in the words of Joseph himself, spoken to his brothers prior to his death: "As for you, you meant evil against me; but God meant it for good, to bring it about that many people should be kept alive, as they are today" (Gen. 50:20).

The second source of moralizing is the use of the old exposition-application scheme. The preacher starts with the exegesis of his text, tries to formulate the message of the text, and then tries to apply this very same message to his own congregation. Since the message has already been fixed before the application, the latter can be little else than a seeking for parallels or analogies in the present situation of the congregation. The most obvious way of doing this is to identify the congregation with the character(s) in the text. Usually it will not be difficult to find some kind of moral parallel.

Now it is not necessarily wrong to identify the people mentioned in the text with the believers of today. As a matter of fact, the Bible itself clearly indicates that the old stories were *also* meant as 'mirrors of identity'. Paul writes about the events of the Exodus and the journey through the desert that "these things are warnings for us, not to desire evil as they did" (1 Cor. 10:6). And concerning God's judgments during the journey through the desert he writes: "Now these things happened to them as a warning, but they were written down for our instruction, upon whom the end of the ages has come" (10:11). In fact we may safely assume that many stories were retained in the oral tradition, because people somehow recognized themselves in these stories. Do we not still have the same experience in our own personal reading of the Bible? Yet we should avoid the mistake of confusing identity with morality. The real point of identity is usually not in the moral aspect of the story but in the aspect of faith and/or unbelief. And the first question we should ask is not: should I act like so and so?, but: how do I, in my situation, respond to God's promises and challenges? May I, in my situation, really accept this promise or does it actually judge and condemn me? Really, our decision about what the message of a specific text is for us depends on a careful analysis of our own situation. It may well be that we, like the exiles in the days of Ezekiel, would love to identify ourselves with the promise of God to Abraham. But have we really the right to do this? Perhaps we should like to identify ourselves with the publican in Jesus' parable of the Pharisee and the Publican. But do we, pious and well-to-do believers of today, have the right to do this? Should we not rather heed the warning of Søren Kierkegaard who once wrote that, from the time that Jesus told this parable, every Pharisee likes to dress as a publican? Again we see how decisive the situation is.

✢   ✢   ✢

There is one more point to be made. This taking into account of the situation as a constituent aspect of the sermon also may be the real answer to the critique of the *monological structure* of the sermon. As we saw in the first chapter, this is one of the main contemporary criticisms of the sermon, which, with its monological structure, is said to be out of keeping with modern dialogical patterns of communication.

In fact, communication theorists believe that communication by its very nature *is* a two-way process. The fifties and sixties witnessed many attempts to find new dialogical forms of preaching. One way is for members of the congregation to share in the preparation of the sermon. During the week a small group meets with the minister to share with him their ideas about and reactions to the text, which he then, one way or another, can incorporate into the sermon.[22] Undoubtedly this can be very effective, when properly handled, but it does not really change the monological structure of the sermon itself. Others, therefore, have tried to incorporate the dialogical element into the worship service itself, by providing the congregation with the opportunity to ask questions after the delivery of the sermon.[23] This too can be very effective, but the sermon itself remains monological in structure.

It was therefore to be expected that others would go a step further and introduce the dialogue into the sermon itself.[24] This has been tried in different ways. One can achieve it by putting two pulpits in the church and arranging a dialogue by two preachers. Or one can allow the members of the congregation to interrupt the preacher by making comments or asking questions. From the various published reports it appears that these experiments generally have been accepted favourably by the congregations. Baumann[25] mentions several values of this kind of preaching. *1.* It produces a high interest level on the part of the congregation. *2.* It helps to clarify issues. *3.* It forces people to face issues that they might otherwise have tuned out. *4.* It deepens faith.

In spite of these benefits, however, the experiments have

[22]Cf. Dietrich Ritschl, *A Theology of Proclamation*, 1960, 123ff., 133ff., 153ff.; Wolfgang Bartholomäus, *op. cit.*, 140ff.
[23]Cf. *Gottesdienst im Gespräch* (ed. by Gerhard Wacker and Paul-Gerhard Seiz), 1969.
[24]Cf. J. Daniel Baumann, *op. cit.*, 259–273; Reuel L. Howe, *Partners in Preaching*, 1967; William D. Thompson and Gordon C. Bennett, *Dialogue Preaching: The Shared Sermon*, 1969; John Thompson, 'When Preaching is Dialogue', *Preaching*, II (1967), 4–13; Hans-Wolfgang Heidland, *Das Verkündigungsgespräch*, 1969; Gottfried Forck, 'Predigt und Gespräch. Zur Homiletik Dietrich Bonhoeffers', in *Brüderliche Kirche – menschliche Welt*, Festschrift for Albrecht Schönherr, 1971, 55–77; M.H. Bolkestein, 'Dialogische Prediking', in *Kerk en Theologie* XII (1961), 1–19.
[25]J. Daniel Baumann, *op. cit.*, 263.

not led to a general replacement of the customary sermon by dialogue preaching. In fact, one hears little about it any more. There are several possible reasons for this. *a.* It is far too time-consuming. *b.* Not every minister can do it. It requires a specific disposition and attitude. *c.* It is questionable whether it is a real solution. Especially when two preachers converse with each other, the people in the church do not get the feeling that they are really engaged in the dialogue. In fact, it is a spectacle rather than a true dialogue. *d.* The interruption of the sermon by comments or questions is not easy either. In large congregations it is virtually impossible, but even in smaller groups it often creates all kinds of psychological problems and tensions.

It is, therefore, not surprising to see that in recent years all these experiments have faded out. As a matter of fact, the question must be asked whether this so-called dialogue preaching touches the heart of the problem. The impression is given that the real problem is the monological *form* of the sermon. Admittedly, this form aggravates the problem. But does not the real problem lie in the *content* of the sermon? This view is supported by an analysis of the complaints of the listeners. Usually they say: "I did not like the sermon today, for what the minister said had nothing to do with my own life, with my worries and frustrations, my questions and doubts, my joys and expectations. What he said may all be very true, but it did not touch me." In other words, the real problem of the sermon as monologue arises when the minister does not succeed in bringing about a real dialogue between the message of the text and the life of the listeners.

Scripture itself teaches us that God's speaking to his people is always dialogical in its very nature. God's revelation to his people is never a proclamation of some abstract, purely objective truth, but God always reveals himself into their active situation. Thus the Old Testament prophets always addressed the people in their concrete historical circumstances. So too, Paul always expounded the significance of the cross and the resurrection of Christ in direct relation to the actual needs of his congregations. Hence the various christological emphases in his letters. Even in the form of his letters we can see the dialogical nature of his approach. He often used the so-called *diatribe* style, a style of discourse which was quite customary among the Stoic street preachers of his day.[26] In it the questions and comments of the listeners were not only anticipated but also clearly formulated and answered by the speaker. A good example of this style in Paul is to be found in Rom. 3: 1–10a. As a matter of fact, the whole letter shows many traces of this style, especially in chapters 9–11, where the apostle deals with the extremely difficult problem of the election of Israel. Keck rightly comments: "By articulating the objections, garnered from experience and formulated trenchantly, Paul took seriously the readers' anticipated responses and acknowledged them openly. More than that, he used them to lead his thinking deeper into his own understanding of the matter." He adds: "In a similar way, today's preacher can articulate openly, and as trenchantly as possible, the anticipated (and known) responses of the people to the text and its theme. This will involve the congregation in the preaching act, and give the sermon a dynamic character as well – a dialogical quality without the artificiality that sometimes attends a 'dialogue sermon'."[27] Of course, one should not fall into the trap of always using the *diatribe* style explicitly. That would be artificial too. Let us remember, it is not the form that is decisive but the content. A sermon, whatever its form, will be really dialogical when it takes the congregation with its joys and sorrows, its questions and doubts, its aspirations and frustrations seriously, by letting the light of God's redemptive Word shine upon them. Preaching that takes account of both the message of the text and the reactions of the congregation and that tries to incorporate these reactions into the exposition of the text will be *truly biblical* preaching and therefore also *relevant* preaching.

---

[26]Leander E. Keck, *op. cit.*, 64f.
[27]*Op. cit.*, 66.

FIVE

Relevant Preaching

When is preaching really relevant? The question follows directly from the two preceding chapters. And the interrogative form is intentional. I know that many people simply *state* that preaching *is* relevant, because it is the preaching of God's Word in Holy Scripture and God's Word is always relevant. The mere statement is not only too easy, even simplistic, but it is also unreal. It does not tally with the experiences of many church people. Too often one hears them complaining that sermons are intensely boring and/or meaningless.

Now a minister can dismiss these complaints by saying that the real problem is not the irrelevance of his preaching, but the unwillingness of his listeners to appreciate its relevance. In other words, it is not his fault, but they themselves are to blame. At worst the minister may even contend that his congregation's unwillingness to listen is fundamentally a matter of unbelief! Such a ministerial reaction, however understandable it may be psychologically, is also too easy and too simplistic. Admittedly, the Bible does speak of the unwillingness of the human heart to accept the gospel of grace. Jesus himself blamed the people of Jerusalem for this very thing when he said: "O Jerusalem, Jerusalem, killing the prophets and stoning those who are sent to you! How often would I have gathered your children together as a hen gathers her brood under her wings, and you would not!" (Matt. 23:37; Luke 13:34). In his letters Paul speaks of the gospel of the cross as a 'skandalon', a stumbling block (1 Cor. 1:23; Gal. 5:11). The sinful human heart rebels against this message of a crucified Saviour. It refuses to be so humiliated and to accept salvation by pure grace. Every preacher has to make allowance for this negative effect of the gospel. But this does not mean that he has the right to see every negative attitude to his preaching in terms of this biblical 'skandalon'. There may also be a skandalon of quite a different nature, namely, a skandalon resulting not from the gospel itself but from the way it is presented. Sadly people do often not even collide with the real stumbling block, because they have already been turned aside by the human stumbling block which the preacher himself puts in their way; for example, by bringing the message in a dull, boring way, or by being virtually unintelligible, or by merely repeating old, pious phrases, which do not allow people to be really confronted by the gospel in all its sharpness and incisiveness.[1] For all these reasons (and many more could be added) preachers should not withdraw behind the biblical notion of the 'skandalon' and hide themselves in innocence; instead they need to look into the mirror and ask themselves in all honesty: is it perhaps my fault that the people fail to see the relevance of the message I bring? Do my pseudo-stumbling blocks perhaps prevent my listeners from reaching the point where the decision of faith or unbelief is made?[2]

If we face these questions honestly we shall be led to recognize that, unfortunately, many such complaints are only too true. Too often we bring the message in such a way

---

[1]Cf. Wilfried Joest, 'Uberlegungen zum hermeneutischen Problem der Theologie', in Praxis Ecclesiae, Festschrift for Kurt Frör (ed. by D. Stollberg), 1970, 20ff.; Paul Tillich, 'Die Verkündigung des Evangeliums', Sammelte Werke, III, 265–275.

[2]In his sermons Calvin often mentioned the necessity for the preacher to bring the gospel message in such a way that the listener will see the relevance of the message. Cf. Pierre Marcel, op. cit., 70f. I quote a few sentences from the forty-fifth sermon on Job: "What advantage would there be if we were to stay here half a day and I were to expound half a book without considering you or your profit and edification?...We must take into consideration those persons to whom the teaching is addressed....For this reason let us note well that they who have this charge to teach, when they speak to a people, are to decide which teaching will be good and profitable so that they will be able to disseminate it faithfully and with discretion to the usefulness of everyone individually".

that people feel: "It's the same old story again. We've heard it so many, many times!" Frequently the minister presents his own, more or less fixed understanding of the biblical message, offering it to a kind of *'homo homileticus'*, a strange, unreal man in the pew whom the preacher himself has invented in the quiet surroundings of his study. Neither the message, nor the person addressed by the message are realities, vibrant with life, but both are familiar abstractions produced in and by the preacher's own mind. Is it any wonder that in such a case the listener fails to see the relevance of such preaching? For – and here we return to territory that has become familiar – the secret of relevant preaching is that the message of the gospel and the situation of the listeners are related to each other in such a way that the listeners discover that this message really concerns their life as it is. *Relevance occurs at the intersection* of the *unique message of the Bible* (cf. Chapter Three) and the *unique situation of the people* in the pew (cf. Chapter Four). Both aspects deserve our further attention.

✵   ✵   ✵

First, we emphasize the *uniqueness of the biblical message*. It is, of course, impossible to summarize this message in a few words. It is so profound and so rich that God himself deemed a whole Bible, consisting of no less than sixty-six books, necessary for his church. Perhaps we shall find as good a summary as possible in some verses from the Epistle to the Hebrews. First, the opening verses: "In many and various ways God spoke of old to our fathers by the prophets; but in these last days he has spoken to us by a Son, whom he appointed the heir of all things, through whom he also created the world" (1:1,2). To this we add a few verses from the fifth chapter: "In the days of his flesh, Jesus offered up prayers and supplications, with loud cries and tears, to him who was able to save him from death, and he was heard for his godly fear. Although he was a Son, he learned obedience through what he suffered; and being made perfect he became the source of eternal salvation to all who obey him" (5:7–9). In these few verses we have the whole biblical message in a nutshell. One could say that the rest of the Bible is virtually nothing else than an almost endless series of variations on this basic theme.

Both parts of this last sentence must be emphasized. There is *one basic theme*, which has to be present in every sermon. Eduard Thurneysen, the close friend of Karl Barth, once put it thus, in opposition to the older liberal theology and preaching of the first decades of this century: "There should be no variety in the sermon. Every Sunday we must say everything and, therefore, every Sunday we must say the same thing .... The church should be the place where Sunday after Sunday the one necessary thing happens, namely that every mouth be stopped, and the whole world be held accountable to God" (Rom. 3:19) ... Sunday after Sunday we should lead all people, including ourselves, into the desert ..., in order that the really last refuge, the only certainty may become visible, in order that God's last and greatest words: forgiveness of sins, the Holy Spirit, mercy, redemption, resurrection, may come from our lips in an authentic way".[3]

Indeed, this is the basic theme of the Bible, but this one basic theme is brought out in almost endless *variations*. Every passage of scripture is a new variation, with its own specific arrangement of the notes and with its own specific tone and timbre. In every passage of Scripture the one great truth of the gospel comes out as a brand-new truth for this particular situation. Admittedly, it is not easy to discover the particularity of the message in every passage. It requires hard and painstaking work. We have to delve into the passage with all the means at our disposal in order to hear the unique variation hidden in the passage.

Unfortunately, it is at this very point that we find one of the great shortcomings of many of us who are preachers. Too often we come to a passage without expecting a new melody at all. We treat the passage almost matter-of-factly, proceed-

[3]Eduard Thurneysen, 'Die Aufgabe der Predigt', in *Die Aufgabe der Predigt* (ed. by Gert Hummel), 1971, 116. The article was originally published in *Pastoral-Blätter für Predigt, Seelsorge und kirchliche Unterweisung*, 63 (1921), 209–219.

ing on the assumption that we already know what it has to say. For we know our Bible, don't we? The natural result of this attitude is that many of our sermons, though based on quite different texts, look as much like each other as leaves from the same tree. Whether our sermon deals with Abraham or Job, Moses or David, it does not really make much difference, for they all have more or less the same face. (Or should we say: they all have become faceless men?) Likewise, it does not make any real difference whether we preach on a text from one of the Synoptic Gospels or from the Gospel according to St. John, whether we preach the message of Paul or of Peter. In all cases the result virtually amounts to the same, timeless message, or as Barth puts it: our preaching becomes "an inarticulate mumbling of pious words".[4]

But let us face it, in this case the fault lies not with the biblical message, but with what we do with it. We turn the message into a timeless truth which is always the same, in whatever time and under whatever circumstances it was revealed. Is it any wonder that our message does not grip our listeners but utterly bores them? Yet the biblical message is *not* a general truth: it is a very particular truth that always appears to be at right angles with our own natural thinking and feeling. It is the strange truth of a God who hates and judges and condemns all sin, and yet loves the sinner and desires him "to be saved and to come to the knowledge of the truth" (1 Tim. 2:4). This truth is ever new again in every new situation. It is like a gemstone with myriads of facets. Even the slightest turn brings out a new and different facet. And because it is a facet of *this* gemstone it is relevant for all men and women of all times. In this respect we can agree with Paul M. Van Buren when he says: "God's Word is life itself. For a world that lies in death, the Word is the resurrection and the life. There can be no question of our making the Word relevant to the world; He did so when He created this world and reconciled it to Himself."[5]

✥   ✥   ✥

[4]Karl Barth, CD, IV, 3, 814.
[5]Paul M. Van Buren, 'The Word of God in the Church', *Anglican Theological Review*, October 1957, 348.

Does this mean that all the preacher need do is to exegete the passage and expound the particular message it contains? As we have seen, the *Barthian tradition* answers this question in the affirmative. Barth himself said it repeatedly in his *Homiletics*. "Preaching should be an exposition of Scripture; the preacher does not have to speak 'on' but 'from' (*ex*), drawing from the Scriptures whatever he says. He does not have to invent but rather to repeat something."[6] Or: "There is, therefore, nothing to be said which is not already to be found in Scripture ... The preacher must accept the necessity of expounding the Book and nothing else."[7] We find the same ideas in the excellent book of Dietrich Ritschl, *A Theology of Proclamation*. As a true Barthian he rejects every suggestion that it belongs to the task of the preacher to relate the message of the text to the situation of the listener. Emphatically he declares that the preacher does not stand as a kind of mediator between the text and the people. He is not the one who has to "get something across". All he has to do is "to observe ... the ... movement ... within the text which is directed to the hearers",[8] for "the sermon text has the self-will to cause the embodiment of God in the assembled congregation."[9]

I believe that this approach is an oversimplification. Certainly the basic idea is sound: the message we have to preach is to be found in the Scriptures. Here we listen to the voice of God's prophets and apostles as they witness to God's self-revelation in the history of Israel and in the

---

[6]Karl Barth, *Prayer and Preaching*, 69.

[7]*Op. cit.*, 89.

[8]Dietrich Ritschl, *op. cit.*, 148.

[9]*Op. cit.*, 147. In his article, 'Der Theologe zwischen Text und Predigt' (republished in *Die Aufgabe der Predigt*, 278–294), Hermann Diem also puts all emphasis on the exegesis of the text. This is so important, even decisive, to him that he dares to say: when the exegete has succeeded in finding the kerygma of the text, he has the 'critical point' of all his endeavours behind him! To illustrate it he uses the picture of a man who wants to learn how to swim and thinks that he has to keep himself afloat by his own movements. But soon he discovers that he can swim only when he allows himself to be carried by the water. So the preacher should allow himself to be carried by the witness of the text (286f.) He has not to worry about the situation of the listener either, or to be concerned with the question whether he is able to 'translate' the message for modern man. He may leave all this safely to the text itself. By its kerygma the text will create the situation in which hearing is really possible(289f.)

history of Jesus Christ. With the church of all ages I believe that these Scriptures are the Word of God, "which contains all things necessary for salvation"[9a] and which, therefore, is relevant for all times. But we may never forget that even in the Bible the Word of God always occurs in a historical situation and context. Although the Word is meant for all times, it never takes the form of a timeless truth. Therefore, our preaching today, in order to be the Word of God for people of today, must be addressed to these people in their concrete historical situation. At this point it is obvious that our twentieth century is vastly different from the first century in which Paul wrote his letters and the evangelists wrote their Gospels, or from the eighth century B.C.in which Amos and Hosea spoke to the people of Israel. Preaching that does not take this *time-gap* into account becomes timeless and may easily "miss the mark".

☆   ☆   ☆

It is evident that we are faced here with a very complex problem that has to be handled carefully. *Two dangers* in particular are to be avoided studiously. The first danger is that of *exaggerating* this time-gap. We find this, for instance, in the writings of *Ernst Lange*. According to him the preacher has to exegete his text very carefully, but then he adds: "What he finds in his exegesis is by no means what he has to preach, not even in this way that he tries to find 'new words' for this historical event (described in the text), words that are intelligible for people of today. For the situations, which in his text are becoming full of promise through the gospel, *belong to the past*. The listeners who in the text are exposed to the effect of the proclaimed gospel, are *not* his listeners".[10] Elsewhere he writes: "The text, as historical text, is a witness to the fact that the Christian tradition becomes relevant in a very definite, *past* situation and as such the text is *fully*

[9a]*Thirty-Nine Articles*, Art. 6.
[10]Ernst Lange, *Predigen als Beruf*, 1976, 64.

relevant for the situation *Hic et Nunc* (here and now)."[11] Now we should not misunderstand Lange. He does not say that the biblical message (or as he likes to call it: the Christian tradition) is not relevant at all. On the contrary, he believes that *every text* speaks of the relevance of this tradition. To him the whole Bible is one long process of this becoming relevant of the biblical tradition in certain historical situations. On this point I think he is right. In the Bible we do find this movement of the revelation becoming relevant in ever new situations. But I cannot agree with his conclusion, namely, that because the texts speak of relevance in past situations the text is consequently "fully irrelevant for the situation *Hic et Nunc*".

This strikes me as an extreme position, which completely ignores that history displays not only discontinuity but also *continuity*. Undoubtedly, there is an element of discontinuity. We see this in particular in the so-called historical texts. But there are also many texts in which the *common* situation of man, before God and in relation to his fellow-man, stands to the fore. In this connection, we could cite many passages from the psalms and the prophets, the Gospels and the Epistles. In them we should find a great deal of direct relevance, enabling the believer of today to recognize himself and his own needs immediately. But even in passages where the discontinuity predominates, there is usually also an element of continuity present in the deeper layers of the text. In his *Biblical Hermeneutics* Karl Frör says concerning the New Testament that there are many analogies between the congregation then and now.[12] Quite often we discover that we face the same needs, temptations, dangers and difficulties. Of course, even then we still have to actualize the message for our present situation, which has its own uniqueness. Frör offers the following poignant formulation: "The situation in which we find ourselves today is unique (German: *einmalig*), inexchangeable, but it is not occurring

---

[11]*Op. cit.*, 42 (my emphasis K R.) Cf. also what he writes on page 28: "What the preacher has to say about the relevance of the tradition for the present *(Hic et Nunc)* is not found in the text".

[12]Kurt Frör, *op. cit.*, 252ff.

for the first time (German: *erstmalig*)."[13] "Despite all the
changes that take place the spiritual situation of the pilgrim
church remains the same. The same gifts nourish her and
the same temptations threaten her. What happened to her
on her way through the ages and what will happen to her in
the future has been announced paradigmatically in the
'preaching book' of the Old and New Testaments. Because of
this deep simultaneity in all change it is possible to bridge
the gap between the preaching of the text and the preaching
of today. And the congregation of today has an immediate
understanding of what was said to the congregation of the
past, because it is addressed by the same Lord and stands in
the same battle of faith."[14]

☆   ☆   ☆

This basic continuity, however, should not cause us to fall
into the other danger, namely, that of *underestimating the
discontinuity*! Frör's formulation is also true when we reverse
it! Although our situation may not be occurring for the first
time (*erstmalig*), nevertheless it still is unique (*einmalig*) and
inexchangeable. Every age has its own questions and problems which in this specific form did *not* occur before. We do
not live in the eighth century B.C. or in the first century A.D.
We live now, in this twentieth century and in our preaching
we have to take this fact entirely seriously. It will not do to
regard the basic problem as a matter of 'language' only. This
is suggested by D. Ritschl, when he says that we should "go
right ahead in our modern way of expression",[15] to which he

[13]*Op. cit.*, 252. Cf. also John Dryden's saying: "For mankind is ever the same and
nothing is lost out of nature, though everything is altered", in 'On the Characters in
the Canterbury Tales', in Preface to *Fables, Ancient and Modern*. I have borrowed
this quotation from Barbara W. Tuchman, *A Distant Mirror*, 1978, where it occurs on
the page after the title page. Her Foreword includes other interesting quotations.
From Voltaire: "History never repeats itself, man always does." From the French
medievalist Edouard Perroy: "Certain ways of behaviour, certain reactions against
fate throw mutual light upon each other." Mrs. Tuchmann herself says: "Qualities
of conduct that we recognize as familiar amid these alien (medieval) surroundings
are revealed as permanent in human nature" (*op. cit.*, XIV).
[14]Kurt Frör, *op. cit.*, 252/3.
[15]Dietrich Ritschl, *op. cit.*, 139.

adds: "Thus we avoid the intellectual complications which arise when the gap of the famous 'two thousand years' between the Bible and the 'modern man' dominates the sermon." To be honest, I wish that it were only a matter of language! In actual fact it goes much deeper.

In the twenty centuries that have passed since the birth of Christ, there have been tremendous changes in our whole culture. Indeed it is a commonplace to say that we in our century are witnessing changes that far surpass the changes of the previous nineteen centuries. Suddenly the old cultural pattern of a society dominated by agriculture and craftmanship has been replaced by that of an industrialized, urbanized society. The consequences are staggering. Instead of being static our culture has become dynamic-functional. Uniformity has given place to plurality, and old-fashioned, patriarchal patterns of authority are rapidly disappearing under the impact of a continuing process of democratization that affects all areas of life. All this suggests that we have arrived at a decisive juncture in our Western civilization; so that every serious preacher must needs take account of the impact produced by all these changes upon the lives of his listeners. He cannot and may not proclaim the biblical message as if we are still living in a cultural climate that is basically similar to that of the New Testament, or even to that of the sixteenth century.

Preachers should perhaps listen more carefully to modern historians. In the preface of her fascinating book on the fourteenth century, A Distant Mirror, Barbara W. Tuchman observes: "People of the Middle Ages existed under mental, moral, and physical circumstances so different from our own as to constitute almost a foreign civilization."[16] A little further on she describes the difference between that time and ours in the following way: "The insistent principle (of the Christian religion) that the life of the spirit and of the afterworld was superior to the here and now, to material life on earth, is one that the modern world does not share, no matter how devout some present-day Christians may be. The rupture of this principle and its replacement by belief in

[16]Barbara W. Tuchman, op. cit., XIV.

the worth of the individual and of an active life not necessarily focussed on God is, in fact, what created the modern world and ended the Middle Ages."[17] I suppose that what Mrs. Tuchman says about the Middle Ages applies, to a large extent, also to the century of the Reformation. In that century too (and also for quite some time afterwards) the Christian religion (with the "insistent principle" mentioned by Mrs. Tuchman) was still "the matrix and law of ...life, omnipresent, compulsory".[18] But all this emphatically belongs to the past. The cultural climate has changed completely, and every preacher should realize that his listeners have been deeply affected by this change. Therefore he should try to speak the biblical message in such a way that his listeners discover that it is of utmost relevance for them in their actual situation in this last quarter of the twentieth century.

Naturally, this does not mean that the biblical message must be *adapted* to this situation. Adaptation implies that the situation lords it over the message and determines what is relevant and what is not. This always leads to a *reduction* of the message, robbing it of its critical power and changing it into a sop that does no more than satisfy the jaded palate of the listener. P.T. Forsyth rightly warned his audience (which mainly consisted of theological students): "We must all preach *to* our age, but woe to us if it is our age we preach, and only hold up the mirror to our time."[19] No, it is not adaptation that we need, but rather what Calvin called 'accommodation'. Calvin used this term again and again in his doctrines of revelation and scripture and meant by it that God in his revelation condescends to our level, in order that we may understand him.[20] R. Bohren has taken up this expression in his homiletics and applied it to our problem. He calls it "the accommodation of the Holy Spirit".[21] Just as in the Incarnation "the Son of God stooped so low as to take upon Himself our flesh, subject to so many miseries",[22] so in

[17]*Op. cit.*, XIX.
[18]*Op. cit.*, XIX.
[19]P.T. Forsyth, *op. cit.*, 5.
[20]Cf. my book *Karl Barth's Doctrine of Holy Scripture*, 1962, 69ff.; Ronald S. Wallace, *Calvin's Doctrine of the Word and Sacrament*, 1957, 2ff.; Werner Krusche, *Das Wirken des Heiligen Geistes nach Calvin*, 1957, 174.
[21]Rudolf Bohren, *Predigtlehre*, 1971, 462.
[22]John Calvin, in his *Commentary on John's Gospel*, Vol. I, 45.

the preaching of the Word the Holy Spirit lets the gospel enter into all kinds of different situations. On each occasion the gospel "accommodates itself" to the hearer in his particular situation, without losing its power or its character of *'skandalon'*.[23] On the contrary, exactly in this accommodation it appears to be the living voice of God, penetrating into the actual life of the listener, yes, into his very heart, the centre of his being.

☆   ☆   ☆

All this is not just a neat theological theory; we see it happening time and again *in the Bible itself*. On pages 66f. we used the examples of Ezekiel and Isaiah. Both used the same tradition, but they used it in quite different ways, and these ways were determined by the situation of their listeners. The truth and, therefore, the relevance of the biblical message is always co-determined by the situation. Exactly in this way God's Word proves to be a word-in-action. It is never static but always dynamic. It is never just 'old-time religion'. On the contrary, it is a Word that is constantly 'on the move'. In fact, the whole Bible is one long record of how God's truth is constantly being *interpreted* and *actualized* in ever new situations. What is even more, the Bible shows us that new situations may cause the 'old' truth to be *re-interpreted* and *re-actualized*, in order to be relevant again for a new, as yet unknown situation. Here are a few examples of this intricate process, taken from both the Old and New Testament.

As far as the *Old Testament* is concerned, we find evidence of this process in all its parts.[24] In the laws of the Pentateuch the most outstanding example is the difference between the two versions of the Decalogue in Exodus 20 and Deuter-

---

[23]Rudolf Bohren, *op. cit.*, 463.

[24]For this section on the Old Testament I have made extensive use of an article by B.J. Oosterhoff, Professor of Old Testament in the Seminary of the Christian Reformed Church in the Netherlands: 'Herinterpretatie in het Oude Testament' (Re-interpretation within the Old Testament), *Rondom het Woord*, XV (1973), 95–117.

onomy 5. Although Exodus 20 explicitly states that God himself spoke these 'ten words', we observe in Deuteronomy 5 that, when they are re-issued before Israel's entrance into Canaan, Moses does not hesitate to make small changes in order to make them fit the new situation of Israel as a settled nation.[25] The same happens in the book of Deuteronomy to the laws of the so-called Book of the Covenant, originally published in Ex. 20:22–23:19.[26] Apparently at a later stage of Israel's history it was felt that these old laws, the principles of which were retained, had to be updated in order to be suitable for a different set of circumstances. Something similar can be observed in some of the psalms, Psalm 51, for instance, undoubtedly was originally a song of individual confession of sin, but by the addition of the verses 18 and 19 the whole psalm became a confession of sin for the whole nation during the exile.[27]

In the prophets too we find examples of re-interpretation and re-actualization of older material for a new situation. Is. 14:1–3 clearly is a later insertion referring to the return from the exile, which means that thus an older prophecy (Is. 13:2 – 14:23), which had its setting in the prophet's own time, has been re-actualized for a new situation. B.J. Oosterhoff even suggests that the idea of re-interpretation and re-actualization may provide the key to the baffling problem of Deutero-Isaiah. He asks: Could the second half of the book be a re-interpretation of old words of Isaiah himself? Could

---

[25]Cf. J.A. Thompson, who in the Introduction to his commentary on *Deuteronomy* (Tyndale Old Testament Commentaries), 1974, writes: "On the view that Moses was responsible for both forms of the decalogue it is not inconceivable that after nearly forty years he would restate some of his principles to suit a new set of circumstances. Alternatively, it has been argued that Mosaic principles set out in the Exodus decalogue were re-expressed at some undefined time after his death in slightly different terms" (*op. cit.*, 29). Likewise M.G. Kline writes: "In covenant renewal documents, modification of the stipulations, and particularly modernization, was customary. That explains the various differences between the Ex. XX and Dt. V forms of the Decalogue. For example, Dt. V. 21 adds 'his field' because of the relevance of land ownership to Israel's now imminent inheritance of Canaan" (article on 'Ten Commandments', in *The New Bible Dictionary*, 1962, 1251).

[26]For a list of parallels, see J.A. Thompson, *op. cit.*, 27.

[27]The same principle applies to the psalms 22 (addition of the verses 27–31), 69 (addition of the verses 30–36), 102 (addition of the verses 12–23), 107 (addition of the verses 2 and 3). It is also very likely that some of the so-called royal psalms received their messianic interpretation after the exile, when Israel no longer had kings (cf. B.J. Oosterhoff, *art. cit.*, 110).

it be a collection of sermons on texts of Isaiah by a prophet during the exile?[28]

Finally, we observe the same process also in the so-called historical books. There can be no doubt that the author of Chronicles made use of the books of Samuel and Kings. Yet he gives a new interpretation. He interprets Israel's history as a theocratic history with two centres: the temple cult and the Davidic dynasty. This view not only serves as the criterion of selection for the material he uses, but it also gives him the opportunity to write in such a way that the history of the past becomes a message for his own day.[29]

When we turn to the *New Testament* we first of all see that the New Testament writers deal in the same way with the Old Testament, their Bible! In a new christological re-interpretation and re-actualization Matthew applies Hosea 11:1, originally referring to the Exodus, to the return of the child Jesus from Egypt. In the Songs of Mary and of Zechariah much old material is applied to the new redemptive situation created by the coming of the Messiah. Likewise in Eph. 4:8ff. Paul re-interprets Ps. 68:18 and applies it to the exalted Christ, who, when he ascended on high, gave gifts to men. While in Acts 4:25 and 26, Psalm 2 is interpreted as referring to Herod and Pilate, who with the Gentiles and the peoples of Israel were gathered against God's holy Servant Jesus.

But this is only one aspect of New Testament re-interpretation and re-actualization. What is even more important is the fact that *within the New Testament itself* we again observe the same process. Take, for example, the Gospels. Each in their own way, the evangelists want to tell the story of Jesus, who is the Christ, or as John puts it quite frankly at the end of his Gospel: "These (things) are written that you may believe that Jesus is the Christ, the Son of God, and that believing, you may have life in his name" (20:31). Obviously these men are not writing as historians or biographers, but as Christian preachers. As such they are natur-

---

[28]*Art. cit.*, 116.
[29]Cf. *art. cit.*, 102ff. Cf. also Edward J. Young, An Introduction to the Old Testament, 1956, 393; P.R. Ackroyd, article on 'Chronicles, I and II', in *IDB, Suppl. Vol.*, 156–158.

ally deeply concerned about the content of their message: it must be a faithful account of the life, death and resurrection of their Lord. But they are no less concerned about the needs of their congregations, who live some forty or more years after the resurrection and ascension of the Lord. In these forty or more years all kinds of developments have taken place and therefore the message about Jesus Christ has to be told in a way that is relevant for the present situation of the congregations. And so in the Gospels themselves we clearly see the beginnings of a new process of re-interpretation and re-actualization.

Here are a few examples from the Gospel of Matthew, the most 'congregational' of all four Gospels. Comparing it with Mark we notice, for instance, that the story of the storm on the sea underwent some remarkable changes. In Mark 4:36–41 the story is little more than a literal account of what happened, with the purpose of proclaiming Jesus as the Lord of nature. The account of Matthew in ch. 8:23–28 has the same purpose, but now it is simultaneously applied to the congregation of Matthew's own day. We see this in the emphasis on the disciples as "following Jesus" (v. 23; cf. 18–22) and addressing him as "Lord" (v. 25) and in the way that the rebuke is changed from "Have you no faith?" (Mark 4:40) into: "O men of little faith" (Matt. 8:26). The original story about Jesus and his disciples has now also become a story about Jesus and the contemporary church. J.C. Fenton's comment on the passage in Matthew makes the point well: "The Church, like the disciples in the boat, is not to fear the persecution of the world; it will not be destroyed. The Lord is present with his Church, and it must believe in him".[30] Very remarkable is also the different use Matthew makes of the parable of the lost sheep, when compared with Luke. In Luke 15 the parable is used as a warning against the Pharisees and scribes (v.2), who criticize Jesus for associating with tax-collectors and sinners. Matthew records the very same parable in ch. 18, a chapter that deals with relations within the Christian congregation. It now becomes a warning against Pharisaism within the congregation itself. Consequently, the point is no longer the conversion of the

[30]J.C. Fenton, *Saint Matthew* (the Pelican Gospel Commentaries), 1963, 130.

one sinner, which causes rejoicing in heaven (Luke 15:7), but the will of the heavenly Father that none of the little ones in the congregation should perish (Matt. 18:14). In the new situation, that of the Christian congregation, the old truth (= the original parable) is being re-actualized. It is now used "to teach care for one another, and particularly for those who have *gone astray* in sin".[31] We find a similar change of setting in the parable of the workers in the vineyard, in Matt. 20:1–16). Without a doubt, this parable too referred originally to Jesus' controversy with the Pharisees over his association with tax collectors and sinners. But by inserting it into a conversation of Jesus with his disciples Matthew now reactualizes it as a message about relationships within the congregation. Very interesting is also the Matthean version of the parable of the great banquet. In Luke 14:15–24 the parable is meant as a warning for the Pharisees (cf. v. 1). In Matt. 22:1–10 we find a slightly different version (e.g. the Kingdom of God is here represented as a marriage feast), but it is clearly the same story and it is still aimed at the Pharisees (cf. 21:45, 46). Matthew, however, adds a new ending about the man who does not have a wedding garment. This may originally have been another parable of Jesus himself,[32] but even so, by adding this part, Matthew re-actualizes the original story with a view to the Christian congregation. Its members may have heeded the call to come to the marriage feast, but this does not yet mean that therefore they are automatically on the safe side. They are asked a new question: Do you really wear the wedding garment? Are you really clothed with the robe of righteousness, i.e. the new life which characterizes those who belong to the Kingdom?

Joachim Jeremias has made an extensive study of the ways in which the parables have been re-interpreted and re-actualized during the process of transmission, cf. *The Parables of Jesus*, 1963. At the close of his discussion of this process he formulates ten "laws of transformation" (113ff.). The intention of his study is to recover the original forms of

[31]J.C. Fenton, *op. cit.*, 296.
[32]So, e.g., R.V.G. Tasker, *The Gospel according to St Matthew* (Tyndale New Testament Commentaries), 1961, 207.

Jesus' sayings. In other words, his work is part of the search for the so-called historical Jesus. "Our task is a return to the actual living voice of Jesus. How great the gain if we succeed in rediscovering here and there behind the veil the features of the Son of Man! To meet with him can alone give power to our preaching" (op.cit., 114).

Personally I am rather sceptical of this search for the historical Jesus. It not only separates the so-called historical Jesus (Jesus as he really was) from the Christ of faith (Jesus as preached by the Early Church), but it also proceeds on the assumption that the real message lies behind our present texts. But we have no other message than the one contained in these texts! This is the message the Holy Spirit has given to the church.

Yet the discoveries Jeremias has made about the process of transformation are of great importance for every preacher, because they can really help him to get a better insight into what the *present texts* want to say. Of course, one must always remain cautious, realizing that there is a strongly hypothetical element in this kind of research. Many New Testament scholars, for instance, believe that there is no clear borderline between the words of Jesus and those of the prophets of the Early Church. They believe that quite often words were put into Jesus' mouth, which in actual fact were utterances of these prophets. In our opinion, such a hypothesis has no foundation in the facts. Cf. William Barclay, *The First Three Gospels*, 1966, 101ff. I agree with Barclay's conclusion "that the Form Critics have done an immeasurable service in enabling us to understand the formation, the genesis and the aim of the gospels, but that their one mistake is their failure to see that the gospel writers sought to awaken faith *by showing Jesus as he was*. This is not to say that they have the standards and the methods and the accuracy of a modern scientific historian, but it is to say that their aim was *to show Jesus as he was in the days of his flesh in order that men might by faith find the Risen Lord*" (op.cit., 115 – my emphasis, K.R.).

☆　☆　☆

It would not be difficult to give many more examples both from the Gospels and also from the Epistles,[33] but it is time to draw some *conclusions for our preaching*. The main conclusion seems to be that the Bible not only warrants but even urges us, when new, as yet unknown situations arise, to preach the biblical message in such a way that our sermon is a re-interpretation and re-actualization of the original message. This statement could, of course, be misunderstood and misused. Some people might find it perilously near the so-called *'life-situation preaching'* advocated by such liberal theologians as Harry Emerson Fosdick.[34] They took their starting point in the needs of their listeners or the issues of the hour, the result being, as Robert J. McCracken, Fosdick's successor acknowledged, that "what is said in church on Sunday frequently has the character of an editorial comment with a mild religious flavour. It lacks any distinctive Christian insight and emphasis".[35] What I mean is quite different from this. I firmly believe that the message the minister has to preach is to be found in his *text*. There, and nowhere else, does he find the *'kerygma'* for his sermon. As the *Second Helvetic Confession* puts it so clearly: "this Word of God", i.e., the Word which we find in Scripture, has to be preached. But – and this is my point – preaching is not just a repetition of the message of the text. The Word that the preacher hears in his text has to be said *anew*. Every sermon should be a *new claim of God* upon the listener of today in his concrete, historical situation. But then, of course, the listener himself, with his experiences and questions, with his faith and his doubts, should also be present in the sermon! For how otherwise will he be able really to hear God's claim on his life?

☆   ☆   ☆

[33]E. G., Paul on divorce, cf. Leander E. Keck, *op. cit.*, 122ff.
[34]Cf. Craig Skinner, *The teaching ministry of the pulpit. Its history, theology, psychology, and practice for today*, 1973, 55ff.
[35]Robert J. McCracken, *The Making of the Sermon*, 1956, 62.

This view of preaching also entails a specific *method of sermon* preparation. Both the traditional method of explication and application, which we still find in many textbooks, and the method advocated by Lange and his friends fall short here. The *traditional* method is virtually a matter of one-way traffic. The preacher's first task is to make a careful exegesis of his text in order to find the content of his message. Having found this he sits down and tries to find ways of applying this message to his listeners. He draws, as it were, lines from the *'kerygma'* of the text to the lives of the listeners. Or to put it in a less kind but perhaps clearer way: he puts the *kerygma* into the wheelbarrow of his sermon and dumps it off at the pews. The method of *Lange* and his friends is virtually the opposite. Taking his starting point in the situation of his listeners, the preacher goes to the biblical tradition as exemplified in the chosen text in order to look there for some meaningful and relevant answers to the questions of the listeners. But the problem of this method is that the function of the Bible is easily limited to answering our questions, while the questions the Bible itself wants to put to us are scarcely heard. The following method should avoid the shortcomings of both other methods. It consists of the following steps.

1. Since the text has the primacy – this is the strong point of the traditional method – we should always *start with the text*. We should read it carefully and do this several times in order to get, so to speak, the 'feel' of the text. We should also try to formulate its message. Naturally, this is only a preliminary formulation, but at this stage we must have some idea of the message.

2. As soon as we think we have succeeded in this, we should reverse the poles and try to look at the text *through the eyes of our listeners*. We should ask ourselves some of the following questions: How will they react to this text and to the message it contains? Will they immediately understand it? Or will they only think that they understand it, while in actual fact they misunderstand it? (Especially in the case of a well-known text the listeners often have their own pre-understanding which may well be a hindrance to a proper understanding.) Will the message please them? Or will it

evoke feelings of resistance or annoyance? And if so, why? The preacher should ask these questions and many more at this early stage of sermon preparation, and he should jot down all the ideas that come to him, even though he may have to discard most of them later on. This second stage may well be the most 'original' and most 'creative' stage in the whole process.

3. Having collected all these ideas the preacher should *turn to the text again*. Now he has to apply himself to the 'hard labour' of careful and painstaking exegesis. Having a general 'feel' of the text is not enough. He has to seek for the special variation on the basic theme that is hidden in this text. But after stage two he does not do it 'tabula rasa' (with a blank slate) any more. Searching for the *original kerygma*, i.e., the message the writer of the text wanted to convey to his original readers, he cannot help remembering the reactions of his own listeners.

4. Once he has found the original *kerygma* he now explicitly *relates* it to these reactions. In some cases it may be that the original *kerygma* gives the direct answer to these reactions. In other cases it may well be that the original *kerygma* is at right angles with these reactions and is severely critical of them. The biblical message is not just a pleasing and comforting message, but often it criticizes and judges us. And to a large extent this is determined by the situation. If Ezekiel had used the Abraham tradition as a comforting message for the unrepentant Jews, he would have strengthened their unbelief and would himself have been a false prophet. It may also be that the original *kerygma* has no direct bearing on the situation of the listeners. Then the preacher may have to do what Matthew did with the parable of the great banquet: go beyond it and carry its movement on until it really intersects with the new situation. No one can say beforehand what has to be done. The preacher has to find it for himself in the process of fulfilling his double task of being representative for both his text and his people.

5. Having discovered what he has to do in this particular instance the preacher should sit down and carefully formulate the *aim of his sermon*. He should try to formulate this aim in one simple sentence: "In this sermon I want to tell the

congregation so and so .... or I aim to motivate them to do this or that ...." Naturally this aim should be in line with the original *kerygma*. To put it in a simple formula: the aim is the *kerygma-in-motion*, namely, moving towards and into the situation, in order to shed the light of God's Word on the situation and/or to challenge and change it, when necessary.

6. When the aim has been clearly defined, the preacher is ready to prepare the *outline* of his sermon and, if necessary, to write the complete sermon.

☆   ☆   ☆

It will be obvious that this method does not make the task of sermon preparation any easier. On the contrary, it becomes more difficult. It means that the preacher must not only be a good *exegete of the Bible* (it is to be hoped that he has learned this in his seminary or college), but he should no less be a careful *exegete of his congregation*. He really has to know his listeners. He has to know who they are and where they are, he has to know what they think and how they are experiencing and coping with all the changes that are taking place, not only around them but also within them. This second kind of 'exegesis' is quite a demanding task. It is really not enough that a preacher regularly reads his newspaper and looks at the T.V. news. He should also be acquainted with contemporary literature and art and with the findings of the social scientists and the psychologists. But above all he should be a faithful pastor who knows his people, who knows what they think and feel. He should know and share their joys and their sorrows, their ambitions and their frustrations, their doubts and their temptations. And in his sermon he should relate the *kerygma* of his text to these actual people. Or to put it in another way: in his sermon he should try to build a *new bridge* between the text and the people. How he has to do this no one can tell him beforehand. No one can give him the exact specifications of the bridge. No method will guarantee sure and quick results. Every sermon is an entirely new venture that requires much creativity on the part of the preacher.[36] He has, one could say, to start building from both banks of the river, and the sermon will be a real bridge only when the two parts meet in the middle.

✣ ✣ ✣

At this point the reader may be inclined to ask: But does it lie *within the power of the preacher* to make the Word of God *effective*? Does this method of preaching, when successful, perhaps guarantee that the Word of God will do its work? The answer must be a loud and strong No! At this point we must take up again the major concern of Karl Barth. Indeed, every preacher should always remember that God is and remains the Subject of his own Word. Man can never and nowhere dispose of the Word of God. However true it may be that preachers of the Gospel are co-workers of God, through whom, as the *First Helvetic Confession (Confessio Helvetica Prior)* puts it, God "imparts and offers to those who believe in Him the knowledge of Himself and the forgiveness of sins, converts, strengthens and comforts men, but also threatens and judges them", we must at the same time affirm with this same confession" that in all things we ascribe all efficacy and power to God the Lord alone, and alone the imparting to the minister. For it is certain that this power and efficacy never should or can be attributed to a creature, but God dispenses it to those He chooses according to his free will"(art. 15).[37] We can also put it in this way: preaching can be properly discussed only within the framework of the *doctrine of the Holy Spirit*. As John Knox says: "True preaching from start to finish is the work of the Spirit."[38] Every preacher should be aware of this and constantly realize that without the Spirit all his efforts amount to nothing.[39] At the same time he should also realize that he

---

[36]Cf. Heribert Arens, Franz Richardt, Josef Schulte, *Kreativität und Predigtarbeit*, 1975.

[37]Arthur Cochrane, *op. cit.*, 105. Karl Barth quotes this article in *CD*, I, 1, 80.

[38]John Knox, *The Integrity of Preaching*, 1957, 89.

[39]Cf. *William Barclay, The Promise of the Spirit*, 1960, 106: "The preacher may be a scholar, a pastor, an administrator, an ecclesiastical statesman, a scintillating orator, a social reformer. He is nothing unless he is a man of the Spirit".

may not reverse this statement and neglect his own respon-sibilities. It belongs to the essence of the Spirit's work that he takes man into his service.[40] This is also the reason why it is so important that we find the right method of preaching. Even though it is true that the Spirit can still do his mysterious work by means of poor preaching, we on our part should do our utmost to find a method that is in conformity with the Spirit's own wish. We believe that the Bible, the Spirit's own book, shows us such a method.

Following the lead given by God himself in his self-revelation as recorded in the Bible, the preacher is called to *relate* the biblical message to the actual life of his hearers. He has to show its relevance in a continuous process of inter-pretation and re-interpretation, of actualization and re-actualization. He has to build the bridge across which the living Word may come and do its wondrous work. Whether the Word will cross the bridge and do its work, whether the listener will *experience* the relevance of the message is beyond the power of the preacher. And let him be thankful for that ! His task is difficult enough as it is! It is a great comfort for every preacher to know that the final decisions are not in his hands, but in those of God himself, who is the sovereign Lord of his own Word and will take care of it.

Preaching is a task given to men who, according to Calvin's well-known saying, are nothing more than "puny men risen from the dust".[41] But these puny men have a promise, which extends even to our twentieth century with all its tremendous changes. It is this promise: "For as the rain and snow come down from heaven, and return not thither but water the earth, making it bring forth and sprout,

---

[40]Cf. what the *Second Helvetic Confession* says in Ch. I: "For although 'no one can come to Christ unless he be drawn by the Father' (John 6:44), and unless the Holy Spirit inwardly illuminates him, yet we know that it is surely the will of God that his Word should be preached outwardly also. God could indeed, by his Holy Spirit, or by the ministry of an angel, without the ministry of St. Peter, have taught Cornelius in the Acts; but, nevertheless, he refers him to Peter, of whom the angel speaking says, 'He shall tell you what you ought to do'" (Arthur Cochrane, *op. cit.,* 225). Here lies one of the basic differences between the work of Christ and that of the Spirit. Christ did his work for us, but without us. The Holy Spirit does his work also for us, but at the same time employs us in his service.

[41]John Calvin, *Institutes*, IV, iii, 1.

giving seed to the sower and bread to the eater, so shall my word be that goes forth from my mouth; it shall not return to me empty, but it shall accomplish that which I purpose, and prosper in the thing for which I sent it" (Is. 55:10, 11).

Appendix

Women in the Pulpit?

During the discussion period after the first lecture at Moore College the question was asked: *"One contemporary criticism of the sermon was omitted in your lecture. There are many who are critical of the fact that preaching is an activity in the church, which is monopolized by men. Is there also truth in this contemporary attack on the sermon?"* I believe that this issue is so important that it should receive attention in this book on preaching. At the same time it is obvious that this attack is of different order from the ones mentioned in Chapter I. It is not an attack on the sermon as an institution, but rather on the tradition which, at least in many evangelical (and catholic!) churches, excludes women from all preaching activities. In our day not only self-professed feminists but many other women as well feel frustrated by this tradition and are beginning to query it.

Scriptural data

But is the Bible not quite clear about the matter? The New Testament knows only male office-bearers. Although it is true that there were many women among Jesus' followers, it is equally true that he chose only men as apostles. In the apostolic church, too, we find men as office-bearers (with the possible exception of female deacons; in Rom. 16:1

Phoebe is called "a deaconess of the church at Cenchreae"[1]; many exegetes, however, are of the opinion that the term 'diakonos' here should not be taken as a technical term for an office-bearer, but rather as an indication of the function Phoebe performed, namely, of attending upon the poor and the sick of her own sex).

Moreover, there are some very straightforward passages, especially in the Pauline Epistles. In I Cor. 11:2–16 Paul speaks at some length about the head-covering of the married woman. She is not allowed to pray or to prophesy with her head unveiled. Emphatically the apostle states that the husband is the head of his wife. Furthermore, the man is the image and glory of God, but woman is the glory of man. In I Cor. 14:34–36 Paul explicitly states that women should keep silence in the churches. They are not permitted to speak, but should be subordinate, as even the law says. If there is anything they want to know, let them ask their husbands at home. For it is shameful for a woman to speak in the church. In Eph. 5:22-33 we again read that the husband is the head of the wife, and therefore the wives must be subject to their husbands in everything. Finally, in I Tim. 2:9–15 it is repeated that the woman must learn in silence with all submissiveness. "I permit no woman to teach or to have authority over man; she is to keep silent".

All these statements are quite unambiguous. There can be no doubt that for Paul the only correct position for a woman was that of subordination to her husband; this had consequences for her place in the assemblies of the congregation: she is not allowed to teach but must keep silent.

A second line of thought

The matter, however, is not as simple and straightforward as it looks. There is still another line of thought in Paul. He speaks not only of subordination but also of reciprocity. In I Cor. 11 we also read: "Nevertheless, in the Lord woman is not independent of man nor man of woman; for as woman

---

[1]Cf. Sister Vincent Emmanuel Hannon S.U.S.C., *The Question of Women and the Priesthood. Can women be admitted to holy orders?* 1967, 71ff.

was made of man, so man is now born of woman. And all things are from God" (vv. 11, 12). In Eph. 5 the passage about the subordination of the women to their husbands is preceded by the exhortation to the whole congregation: "Be subject to one another out of reverence for Christ" (v. 21). Paul even knows of fundamental equality. In Gal. 3:27, 28 he writes: "For as many of you as were baptized into Christ have put on Christ. There is neither Jew nor Greek, there is neither slave nor free, there is neither male nor female; for you are all one in Christ".

It is quite obvious that Paul's thinking on the matter is rather complex. At times it even looks contradictory. Every student of Paul's writings has to face the question of how to reconcile these two lines of thought. It certainly will not do to solve the problem by taking just one line and ignoring the other. Unfortunately this happens too often. Traditional theology is always inclined to take the first series of texts as decisive and to bypass the second line, by declaring that texts such as Gal. 3:27, 28 speak of *spiritual* equality only (i.e., equality before God), but have nothing to do with office or preaching. Modern theology is inclined to take only Gal. 3:27, 28 as decisive and to see the other texts as merely time-conditioned. The whole idea of subordination is regarded as a matter of expediency for Paul, a kind of accommodation to the cultural pattern of that day. Both solutions, however, are too simple. Neither of them does full justice to Paul. Not only was he a very consistent thinker, but we are also faced with the fact that more than once both lines of thought occur in the same passage. It is therefore necessary to look very carefully at the issue in all its complexity.

The cultural pattern of Paul's time

It may be helpful if we first briefly examine this pattern, for it is evident that Paul wrote his letters against the background and within the framework of his own time. All his letters were occasional writings which dealt with concrete issues present in the congregations.

It is a well known fact that in New Testment times the woman as a rule had a very subordinate place, both in the family and in society. As to her place in the ancient Greek family, Sister Vincent Emmanuel Hannon writes: "Both by custom and by law woman was under the authority and control of her father or husband. In the seclusion of the *gynaikonites* she played a respected role, but in almost complete ignorance, with no other occupation than monotonous domestic duties, with the poor compensation of absolute dominion in only a very limited sphere. On marriage she passed from the seclusion of her father's house to similar quarters in her husband's, where she lived as an unequal partner. At best this would be favourable to domestic existence, but the husband's concubinage and intercourse with hetaerae [courtesans, mistresses] coexisted, apparently without weakening domestic relation."[2] As to her place in both family and society, N.J. Hommes writes: "A woman was little more than doll and slave, hidden in the women's quarters, excluded from political and social activity. She was entirely at the mercy of parents, brothers and husband."[3] These words describe the Greek situation. In Roman society matters on the whole were better. Although legally regarded as a mere piece of property in the possession of a husband, women enjoyed considerable freedom and importance.[4] Learning, for instance, was open to them, and we know that many Roman matrons played important parts in politics and literature. Especially in Asia Minor women took a prominent part in public activity, in particular as (high-) priestesses.[5] At the same time there was, in New Testament times, a widespread moral decline, which was marked by the growing prevalence of divorce and by the disintegration of family life. Derrick Sherwin Bailey describes it as follows: "Gradually infiltrating into Roman society, the baser elements of Greek sexual life undermined the severe puritanism of the early tradition, and produced a parody of the spontaneous naturalism of Hellenic sensuality in the coarse, brutal, and calculated vice for which the imperial city has ever since remained notorious. While stricter morals con-

---

[2]*Op. cit.*, 51.
[3]N.J. Hommes, *De vrouw in de kerk*, 1951, 81.
[4]Sister Hannon, *op. cit.*, 58.
[5]*Op. cit.*, 56.

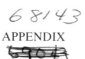

tinued to prevail in many of the provinces where the former
ideals of marriage and family life were preserved, the cities
and ports of the Mediterranean seaboard rivalled or in-
structed the capital in licentiousness."[6])

It is against this background that we have to read Paul's
letters. It explains, for instance, why in his letters to the
congregation at Corinth he writes so much about the position of the woman and about sexual matters in general.
"Corinth had been the centre of profligacy perpetrated in
the service of Aphrodite, where at one time a thousand
female hierodules surrounded the shrine. This degrading
licence in the name of religion was equalled only by the
idolatrous worship of Diana at Ephesus."[7] It was not
without reason that the Greeks had coined the verb 'to
corinthianize', which meant: to go on a spree, to paint the
town red!

In this cultural climate the Christian message that in
Christ there is neither male nor female meant a tremendous
change. In Christ man and woman are equal! But this could
easily lead to new extremes. The Christian gospel of freedom was constantly in danger of being misinterpreted in the
prevailing libertine atmosphere. As a matter of fact, Paul's
letters give the impression that this actually happened.
Some newly converted Corinthians fell prey to such abuses
as incest and fornication, as if there were no limit to the new
freedom (cf. I Cor. 5:1–5; 6:12–20). Some married women
were apparently inclined to behave in the assemblies of the
congregation in a manner which seemed to be unbecoming to
women of their status. They prayed and prophesied with
their heads uncovered, i.e., without wearing a veil (I Cor.
11:5). During the discussions at the teaching/preaching
services some of them monopolized the conversation (I Cor.
14:34, 35) and were bent on teaching the men a lesson or two
(I Tim. 2:12). In other words, they were Christian feminists
before the word was invented.

In this situation Paul had to give leadership to the
congregations. He did it in a very specific, concrete way. He
did not write treatises about the relation husband-wife or

[6]Derrick Sherwin Bailey, *The Man-Woman Relation in Christian Thought*, 1959, 4.
[7]Sister Hannon, *op. cit.*, 105.

Lincoln Christian College

about the place of the women in the congregation, giving a full and balanced exposition, but in each case he gave concrete instructions which applied directly to the local situation. Naturally, we have to take these instructions seriously, but we should also realize that they have to be read within the framework of that particular time and particular stage of development in the Christian church.

Paul's view

When we try to summarize Paul's view, there is no doubt in my mind that his starting point is the fundamental equality of both sexes. This is the startling new element in the Christian message:'in the Lord' or 'in Christ' husband and wife are equal before God! Paul makes this clear in two passages. First, in I Cor. 11: 11,12, where he says: "Nevertheless, *in the Lord* woman is not independent of man nor man of woman; for as woman was made of man, so man is now born of woman. And all things are from God". Most commentators agree that "whatever God arranged at creation when He made man the head, as far as being 'in the Lord' is concerned both are altogether equal".[8] Herman Ridderbos says it even more forcefully: "It is not said here that 'in the Lord' marriage has received another destiny than it had by virtue of creation; it is said, however, that in the Lord the principle of reciprocity, mutual dependence and service to one another in love, applies and comes to effect in a new way".[9] The second passage is Gal. 3:27 and 28, where Paul says that there are not two classes of Christians: a higher class, namely, the men, and a lower class, namely, the women. "As many of you as were *baptized into Christ* have put on Christ" (v. 27). Consequently the Jew has no inherent privileges over the Greek. The free man has no inherent privileges over the slave. The man has no inherent privileges over the woman. They are *all* one *in Christ* and therefore equal before God. As baptized Christians they *all* share in the gifts of the Spirit, the so-called charismata.

[8]R.C.H. Lenski, *I and II Corinthians*, 1946, 446.
[9]Herman Ridderbos, *Paul. An Outline of his Theology*, 1975, 307.

Women, too receive the gift of prophecy and pray in the company of the believers (I Cor. 11:5).[10]

But it is equally clear that Paul nevertheless accords a specific place to the woman, in both the family and the congregation. In both cases it concerns *married* women. According to Paul there is a certain 'order' in the family: the man is the head of the wife (and therefore of the family) and the woman is subordinate to her husband and has to be subject to him. The same idea he applies to the assemblies or worship services of the congregation. The woman must be silent, for she should remain subordinate (I Cor. 14:34). She should learn in silence with all submissiveness and not teach or have authority over men (I Tim. 2:12).

At this point Paul closely adheres to the cultural climate of his time, and he seems to do it quite deliberately. We see this also in the case of slavery. He neither approves nor rejects it. He accepts it as a factual situation and exhorts the believers to behave as believers *in* this factual situation. Although there is the fundamental break-through of equality in Christ, the apostle makes no attempt to revolutionize the existing cultural and social patterns.

Does this mean that the headship of the man and the subordination of the woman within the family is a cultural phenomenon only and that we can ignore it, because it no longer fits in with our cultural situation? This conclusion would be too simple. Again we must say that Paul's view is much more complex.

Arguments

When we study the arguments used by Paul (it should be noted that he never deals with his congregations in a

[10]This seems to imply that the commandment of silence in I Cor 14 and I Tim. 2 cannot be taken absolutely, unless one assumes that the apostolic church had two different kinds of worship services, one in which the women were allowed to pray and to prophesy, another in which they had to be completely silent. Or one has to assume that this verse does not refer at all to assemblies of congregations but to "other opportunities" (so Lenski, *op. cit.*, 437) or "other possibilities" (so F.W. Grosheide, *Commentary on the First Epistle to the Corinthians*, 1953, 251). Most commentators, however, favour the idea that 'praying' and 'prophesying' here does refer to the worship services (cf. I Cor. 14:26–33) where prophecy is mentioned as one of the regular elements in the worship service of the apostolic church).

high-handed way but always treats them as mature people!),
we see that in the various passages he uses arguments of
different kinds. Actually there are three kinds of arguments.

a. *A Christological argument.* In I Cor. 11 this is the starting
point of the whole passage: "The head of every man is
Christ, the head of a woman is her husband, and the head of
Christ is God" (v. 3). With the exception of God, no one is
autonomous, not even Christ. We find a similar argument in
Eph. 5: "For the husband is the head of the wife as Christ is
the head of the church, his body" (v. 23). The emphasis,
however, is slightly different. The relationship between
husband and wife has its analogy in the relationship between Christ and his church. Nevertheless, there is a clear
'order', just as in I Cor. 11.

b. *An argument from creation.* We first find this in I Cor.
11:8 and 9, where Paul writes: "Man was not made from
woman, but woman from man. Neither was man created for
woman, but woman for man". This same argument returns
in I Tim. 2: "Adam was formed first, then Eve" (v. 13), to
which is added a reference to the story of the Fall: "And
Adam was not deceived, but the woman was deceived and
became a transgressor" (v. 14).

c. *An argument from culture.* Several times Paul uses this
argument. E.g., in I Cor. 11:6–15 – "it is disgraceful..." (v. 6);
"is it proper...?" (v.13); "does not nature teach you...?" (v.
14); "it is degrading..." (v. 14). Also in I Cor. 14:35 – "it is
shameful...".

The weight of these arguments

How shall we estimate the weight of these arguments? It
seems to be evident that the first two arguments, which are
of a *theological* nature, constitute the real core of the apostle's
view. According to him, in creation God has established a
definite order for the relationships within marriage: the
husband is the head of the wife and the wife is subordinate
to her husband. In the work of re-creation in Jesus Christ
this order has not been abolished. To be true, husband and
wife are fully equal in their relationship to Christ and to God
(I Cor. 11:11, 12; Gal. 3:28; cf. also I Pet. 3:7 – "joint heirs of

the grace of life"), but the basic order within marriage, as established at creation, remains inviolate. I believe that this idea of a definite order is the lasting element in Paul's view of marriage.

At this point there is a distinct difference when compared with his view of slavery. Feminists often overlook this. They point out that later on the Christian church rejected slavery, in spite of the fact that Paul seems to have accepted it as a matter of course (cf. I Cor. 7:17–24; Philemon). Why then, they ask, should we today not reject his view of the headship of the man as well? They seem to overlook that nowhere Paul grounds the subordination of the slave to his master on the creation order. But in the case of the headship of the man and of the subordination of the woman within marriage he does just that, and if we wish to abolish it, we must realize that we contradict the apostolic doctrine at this point.

Nevertheless, the theological arguments do not solve every problem. The question still remains of how we should express this headship of the man and this subordination of the woman in actual practice. At this very point the *cultural* argument appears to play an important part in Paul's reasoning. He himself formulates the relationship from the perspective of the cultural situation of the period. Apparently he does not wish the women of the congregation to create a stir by their behaviour but admonishes them to be "quiet" and "submissive", terms which were very common in those days. To describe the process N.J. Hommes uses the following illustration: "As the colour of a river is co-determined by that of its bed, so the colour of the New Testament message about the woman is co-determined by its 'bed' in the ancient world".[11] Herman Ridderbos virtually says the same thing, but in a more theological fasion: "The deeper motive, i.e., the place that from the beginning God chose to ascribe to woman in her relationship to man, therefore finds its concrete form in the manner in which it is proper according to custom that a woman conduct herself in public and is to know her place with respect to man....It is clear that there is

[11]N.J. Hommes, *op. cit.*, 159.

... a relativizing element in this appeal to custom and the 'commune measure', insofar, that is, as the (sub-*ordinate*) position of woman with respect to man is to be given expression in a manner that must be considered appropriate for a certain time and culture".[12]

Consequences

All this has important consequences for our present situation. In the first place, for the relation man-woman in the *family*. From the cultural point of view our situation is quite different from that in Paul's days. Even when we recognize that the *basic order* of headship-ordination still applies, we must at the same time admit that the *shape* of this order has changed drastically. Today, at least in our Western culture, marriage is basically experienced in terms of *partnership*, i.e. husband and wife regard and accept each other as partners who both share the full responsibility for the success (or failure) of their marriage.

But there are also consequences for the place of the woman in the *congregation*. In our Western culture it is not "disgraceful" or "improper" for a woman to speak at a congregational meeting or in a mixed adult Bible class. As a matter of fact, we should find it extremely strange, to say the least, if at a congregational meeting or a Bible class the women literally kept silent. Even very traditional churches have accepted this! The whole cultural climate has changed (and let us not forget that this was largely due to the impact of Christianity itself!). But we cannot stop at congregational meetings or Bible classes, but must extend this principle also to the worship services of the church. Here, too, we cannot avoid the task of determining what in our day the place of the women should be, in accordance with the cultural patterns of our time. Undoubtedly, we shall reach different decisions from those reached by Paul. This is not a matter of disobedience or a lack of loyalty. As a matter of fact, I am convinced that Paul would approve of such an action. Our real problem may be that we do not have a clear understanding of the cultural situation in the apostolic church. At that

---

[12]Herman Ridderbos, *op. cit.*, 462, 463.

time the headship of the man did not allow for any position of authority for the woman, in whatever sphere of life. Such a position of authority would threaten or even destroy his headship.

In our culture this is quite different. In an American paper on this subject I recently found the example of a woman being principal of a high school, while her husband worked in the same school as a janitor. This may be an extreme example, but it is certainly not impossible in modern society. Does this mean that in this particular case the husband is no longer the head of the family? When relationships in the family are healthy, this is not at all necessary. The same is true of the royal family. Even though Queen Elizabeth is the head of the United Kingdom, this need not exclude the headship of Prince Philip in the family. There is a story about Queen Victoria and Prince Albert which nicely illustrates our point. One day they had a quarrel and Albert withdrew into his own private rooms. A few hours later Victoria knocked at his door. When he called out: "Who is there?", she replied: "The Queen". The door remained locked! When a little later she knocked again and he repeated his question, she answered: "Your wife." This time he opened the door and the quarrel was soon patched up.

What about the pulpit?

Does all this include the possibility that women engage in preaching activities? I believe the answer can only be affirmative. In our culture no one objects any longer to women addressing public meetings. As a matter of fact, we find this quite normal. For the very same reason no one will call the church revolutionary (Paul's great fear!), if it ordains women and allows them to preach the Word of God. On the contrary, the church may well be in danger of putting up unnecessary obstacles for the progress of the gospel, if she perseveres in her attitude of barring women from the pulpit (and from ordination). Again I venture to say that it is a safe assumption that Paul, if he were alive today, would encourage the church to accept women for the teaching ministry (and ordination), and that he would do it *for the very same reason* which in his own time he put forward against the idea. Today he presumably would say: "Brethren, it is *not proper* that we ignore the gifts of the women, seeing that they make such a great contribution in almost every sphere of life".

Paul was certainly not anti-feminist in the modern sense of the term. It never was his intention to hold women in tight control at all costs. His upholding of the creation order in the family did not mean that in his eyes the man was the 'boss'. On the contrary, he exhorted the men to love their own wives as their own bodies (Eph. 5:28) or as themselves (v. 33; cf. also Col. 3:19). He even said that in the Lord they are both equal! Paul most certainly was no misogynist. More than any of the other apostles he made use of the gifts and services of women in the congregations, also for the spreading of the gospel (cf. Rom. 16:1,6,12; Phil. 4:2). It is striking how many women are mentioned in the list of greetings in Rom. 16. Paul must have had a good relationship with women. They, on their part, must have liked him. I think they saw him as the man who stood up for and protected their position. Today we may feel that his words in Eph. 5 about the headship of the man and the subordination of the women are harsh and unacceptable, but I am sure that the women of Ephesus rejoiced when they read: "Husbands, love your wives, as Christ loved the church and gave himself up for her....Even so husbands should love their wives as their own bodies. He who loves his wife loves himself...Let each one of you love his wife as himself" (Eph. 5:25, 28,33).

What a world of difference there lies between these words and the notorious remark ascribed to the Greek orator Demosthenes: "We keep hetaerae for the sake of pleasure, concubines for the daily requirements of the body, wives to bear us legitimate children and to be faithful guardians of our households!"[13]

---

[13]Demosthenes, Against Neaera, par. 122.

INDEX OF NAMES

Ackroyd, P.R. 86
Albert, Prince 107
Ambrose 17
Ammer, H. 49
Arens, H. 94
Augsburg Confession 33, 38
Augustine 16

Bailey, D.S. 101
Barclay, W. 89, 94
Barr, J. 40f., 52
Barth, K. 1f., 11f., 34ff., 38, 40, 55ff., 63, 76ff., 94
Bartholomäus, W. 6
Bastian, H.D. 5, 9, 12
Baumann, J.D. 10, 15, 70
Beecher, H.W. 10
Belo, F. 51
Bennett, G.C. 70
Bizzard, S.W. 7
Bohren, R. 83f.
Bolkestein, M.H. 70
Bonhoeffer, D. 5
Brown, H.C. 16
Brunner, E. 2f.
Bullinger, H. 33ff.
Bultmann, R. 2

Calvin, J. 7, 17, 32, 74, 83, 95
Carey, W. 17
Chrysostom 16
Clévenot, M. 51
Clinard, H.G. 16
Clowney, E.P. 55
Cochrane, A. 28, 40, 94f.
Confession of 1967 38
Cullmann, O. 52

Danielsmeyer, W. 39
De Boer, P.A.H. 50
De Fraine, J. 50
Demosthenes 108
Den Heyer, C.J. 51
Dibelius, M. 21
Diem, H. 78
Dietrich, G. 51
Dodd, C.H. 19, 24
Dominic 17

Drummond, H. 17
Dryden, J. 81

Ebeling, G. 2, 12, 16,18, 60
Eichrodt, W. 22

Fascher, E. 21
Fenton, J.C. 87f.
Fiore, Q. 8
Forck, G. 70
Forsyth, P.T. 1, 39, 83
Fosdick, H.E. 90
Francis of Assisi 17
Friedrich, G. 20, 26
Frör, K. 48f., 74, 80f.
Fuchs, E. 2
Fuller, R.H. 22
Fürst, W. 60

Goddijn, W. 5
Graham, W. 17
Grasso, B. 19
Grosheide, F.W. 103

Haldane, R. 17
Hannon, V.E. 98, 100f.
Hartwell, H. 34
Heidelberg Catechism 27f.
Heidland, H.W. 70
Helvetic Confession, First 94
Helvetic Confession, Second 33ff., 37, 39, 90, 95
Hippolytus 19
Hoekstra, T. 38
Hommes, N.J. 100, 105
Howe, R.L. 70
Hummel, G. 3, 76

Jeremias, J. 88f.
Joest, W. 74
Jones, I.T. 7, 9f.

Keck, L.E. 5f., 41, 45f., 48f., 64f., 72, 90
Killinger, J. 15
Knox, D.B. 38
Knox, J. 94
Krusche, P. 12

Krusche, W. 83
Kuitert, H.M. 54

Ladd, G.E. 43
Lange, E. 12, 61ff., 79f., 91
Lenski, R.C.H. 102f.
Litton, E.A. 38
Luther, M. 17, 32, 47, 49

McCracken, R.J. 90
McDonald, J.I.H. 24
Machovec, M. 48
McKelway, A.J. 63
Maclaren, I. 17
McLuhan, M. 8
Marcel, P. 38, 74
Marshall, I.H. 43
Marxsen, W. 39, 66
Massey, J.E. 16
Matthiae, K. 65
Moltmann, J. 2
Moody, D.L. 17
Muratorian Canon 19f.
Murphy-O'Connor, J. 19
Murray, J. 31

Niebergall, A. 3, 32
Northcutt, J.J. 16
Nyberg, K. 16

Oosterhoff, B.J. 84ff.
Oswald, E. 67

Packer, J.I. 23
Pannenberg, W. 2, 47, 53
Parker, T.L. 32
Perroy, E. 81

Randolph, D.J. 15
Reid, G. 4, 8ff.
Richard, P. 51
Richardson, A. 54
Richardt, F. 94
Ridderbos, H. 27, 29f., 52, 102, 105f.
Ristow, H. 65
Ritschl, D. 70, 78, 81f.
Robertson, D. 50
Rössler, D. 12
Runia, K. 25, 28, 35, 43, 83
Ryle, J.C. 38

Sanders, J.N. 67

Sankey, I.D. 17
Savonarola, G. 17
Sweazey, G.E. 3, 15f.
Schelsky, H. 5
Schweizer, E. 3
Schweitzer, A. 47
Schlier, H. 31
Schönherr, A. 70
Schulte, J. 94
Scott, M.L. 9
Seiz, P.G. 70
Skinner, C. 90
Sölle, D. 13
Spurgeon, C.H. 17
Steffensky, F. 13
Stollberg, D. 74
Straver, C.J. 11

Tasker, R.V.G. 88
Thirty-Nine Articles 38, 79
Thompson, J. 70
Thompson, J.A. 85
Thompson, W.D. 70
Thurneysen, E. 76
Tillich, P. 2, 62f., 74
Tuchman, B. 81ff.
Tucker, G.M. 41, 44, 49

Van Buren, P. 2, 77
Van Trigt, F. 50
Via Jr., D.O. 50
Victoria, Queen 107
Vogelsanger, P. 3
Voltaire 81
Von Rad, G. 23, 52, 55
Vriezen, Th.C. 23

Wacker, G. 70
Wallace, R.S. 83
Weiss, K. 65
Wesley, J. 4, 17
Westermann, C. 53, 55
White, R.E.O. 10, 17
Whitefield, G. 4, 17
Winter, F. 49
Wood, A.S. 32
Worley, R.C. 24
Wright, G.E. 22, 52

Young, E.J. 86

Zwingli, H. 33

251

R 943

68143